Let's un-Do This

Rewrite Your Story to Live Life Fully Awake

Riley Sloan Powell

Butterfly Books Publishing

Sweet friend,

As you embark on this journey with me, I want to invite you to delve into your story as I share mine.

I'm offering you a gift to guide you in digging deeper and finding God's voice in your own life. How He uniquely talks to you!

This journaling workbook isn't like any other you've encountered, and I know it will be so worth it for you.

Get your gift at: *rileysloanpowell.com/gift*

Let's undo this and rewrite our stories together!

What Others Are Saying:

"'*Grand things happen on the car rides and with the friends.*'
If you're like me, and you really think about it, many of your favorite moments have likely taken place in the car. On road trips or Target trips, with friends or alone, the car is our studio, our stage, our sanctuary. It is literally and figuratively our vehicle for exploring the world.
Let's un-Do This is a spontaneous invitation to a road-trip with your best friend. It's the trip you blurt "YES!" to, without overthinking, because you know these are the moments that change you, fill you, move you into being and doing. Each chapter of Riley's memoir feels like singing loudly and laughing wildly while exploring hidden places with your bestie. It is secret-sharing, tears together, and the healing that comes when a trusted friend can replace our lived-in lies with God's personal, intimate truth. Intimacy is the goal, and we can find that in these pages, investing ourselves in a shared story. Riley's voice is fully present from the driver's seat, whispering her own fragile story and declaring her delight, so that we might feel connected, known, forgiven, invited into our own resurrection. So that layers of our own hearts may be returned through divine friendship that leads us to Jesus." – Summer Morrell

"Riley's detailed storytelling immerses readers into personal moments of her life, leaving a longing for more. Through her unapologetic sharing, she encourages us to find God in our stories, emphasizing His presence can be known by anyone willing to seek and embrace it. Riley reminds us that we are HUMAN and that when we allow ourselves to see the delight that God takes in us it has the ability to inspire a profound sense of renewal. The book leaves you feeling alive and ready to rewrite your own story by openly making space for God's presence." – Sarah Bilger

"Riley Sloan Powell's voice sounds a clarion call though her new book *Let's unDo This.* Part memoir, part call to action, this book is her earnest anthem to readers who are lost in the fog of searching for perfection, or anticipating greener grass with the proper Pinterest board. She leads us through her search for spiritual connection and peace into her accidental stumble upon herself in a wholly unexpected way. Powell is fearless in her ability to lay bare the beauty, the fear, the pain and the courage of her journey. Her prose is engaging, enthusiastic and full of passion. Our reward is a story full of lessons of finding yourself and the true meaning of life in unexpected places and ways and perhaps a road map to begin our own journey. Bravo Riley." – Andrea Trussler Storie

Let's un-Do This: Rewrite Your Story to Live Your Life Fully Awake
Copyright © 2024 Riley Sloan Powell
First Edition Published by Butterfly Books Publishing

Cover Design by Chloe Zola
Interior Design and Typesetting by Katelyn Silva
Edited and Proofread by Jake Waller.

ISBN (paperback): 979-8-9893615-5-7
ISBN (hardcover): 979-8-9893615-6-4

Printed in the United States of America.

The events and conversations in this book have been set down to the best of the author's ability, although some names and details have been changed to protect the privacy of individuals.

www.rileysloanpowell.com

Table of Contents

Acknowledgments

I'd like to give the biggest thanks first to Elsa, Anna, and Elphaba for leading the way in forging brave paths. Those are my girls.

My sweet Baby Grey, thank you for that conversation on the stairs that gave me the courage to start. Thank you for every car talk, porch talk, late night chat on the kitchen counter where you gave yourself fully. Your calm and present demeanor makes every person feel so loved, especially me. You have a gift for seeing and feeling that is beyond expectation. Thank you for adding the color blue to "Jesus Loves the Little Children." It changed me. You change me. I wrote this because you believe in me.

Mama, there may not be a chapter with your name at the heading but that does not for a second diminish your monumental contribution to my story. You planted every seed. You nourished and cared and protected. There is not a single page where you are not woven into the details. Every one is covered by your love. No one knows me as deeply as you do and I know your heart has broken with mine countless times. You could probably have written this book for me! You promised victory and showed me the way to dig deep and seek out truth. Thank you for being the perfect mom for me. I hope this dream come true brings you delight.

Daddy, your voice is forever my guiding light. Our connection doesn't require words. Your strong presence has sustained me through all of life's chapters. I could because you said so. You erase my fear. You speak life into my future. I promise not to weave in and out of cones. Thank you for trusting me. Thank you for showing me the way.

My Joshua, what can I say to honor you? How can I possibly reflect the magnitude of who you are to me? You rescued me. You rescue me still. We take all that could be wrong and choose to make it beautiful. A story of restoring over and again. You choose better and show me the way. It shows up in the steady way you give. It shows up in kitchen cleaning parties. You bring delight to our home. I am in awe of the way you desire more for life, more for our kids. Your gift is calling people higher. Thank you for every take out order and for every dish washed, there must have been 5 million. Every time I worry and overthink, you say, "we're good, Riley." Being loved by you is my greatest gift. I wrote this to make you proud.

Keean, you see bigger! You see brighter! You dream and create and believe that best is possible. You keep it real and force me to be present. You magically create joy when you see I'm overwhelmed. Thank you for every heart you've given: the Lego one, the wooden one you carved, the rock, the Tinkertoy...you see life in so many things and give it away to bring delight. Thank you for holding the branches back on our walks. Thank you for every peck on the cheek and every tickle war. I wrote this to show you dreams come true.

Ivy, my darling girl, thank you for showing me that creation comes in open spaces of surrender. You've taught me that as I am emptied and broken, I am nourished perfectly. In the darkness, snuggled heart to heart with you, is where these words were birthed. Our time together has healed my need for anything other than what is right here in front of me. I wrote this for your legacy.

To Katelyn, you are so much more than my book coach. You were gifted straight to me from God. You have become my friend and confidante. The way you serve others in your gifting is changing the world. I am beyond in awe of how you calmly make space for my spastic word vomit then with simple words of truth guide me to a place of abiding in Jesus and creating. We just need to note the miraculous.

I must give thanks to my Savior, my Jesus. He started as my parents'. I saw Him beautiful in others. He shows up in so many awe inspiring ways and I just wanted that for myself. I wanted all of it! I wanted the goodness. I wanted the peace. I wanted the courage and confidence and assurance that it is well. I wanted the boldness to defend something so true. I wanted the pure love that spread to others with ease. Jesus, over and over, patiently and with such tenderness, has taken away heaviness and shown me how to breathe. He has told me that love covers my story. He has shifted my eyes from my own sorrows into a love for life and others. He says it is good. You are good. Let it be easy. Now He is mine and I am His. Settled and good. No striving or worry or exhaustion. Just comfort and rest from the world in His presence. There is nothing like it.

I want to thank each friend mentioned in this story, and honestly, so many who aren't, but are just as valuable. Your courage to let me use your name speaks to the immense character you hold. The love of Jesus spills from your life in every big and small way you live your days. I am in awe of each of you. Thank you for holding space for me and for loving me with such beautiful grace. But let's be real, I'm mostly thankful for fits of laughter and good food. Thank you for distracting me with fun and for keeping life sane. The nitty gritty day-to-day is where the real stuff happens and I'm so thankful to have you by my side. I know God because of seeing Him in you.

Prologue

Hey, hey, hey! Come in, come in! I want you here.

Sweet friend. Sweet human. Sweetest child of God. You are loved here! What if we came into this space and took a deep breath in and blew out every piece of our stress and worry and fear? What if we could step into a reality that feels light and without noise for a moment?

Let this space be easy. There is grace to walk in deep places. Let us be a people who are settled on what is good and true, unmoved by things that shift in our lives. In these spaces, we put our weight on our foundation. How would we feel? Who could we be if we weren't carrying so much heaviness?

This space is learning to be there, learning to find the quiet, building a foundation that holds you. Breathe deeply and know it is good. He created you and with delight said you are so so so good.

I spent an unbearable amount of time hating my story. Is that my life? Is that myself? It feels weird to say it like that... feels slightly dramatic. At the time, I didn't even know I felt that way!

I've always been really friendly; never been one to feel depressed or negative. In fact, I love life a lot! I make every moment a celebration. I've always had a great time and seen the best in every moment. I will only allow a moment—two is extreme—in a day to be considered "bad", never summing up a whole day as dreadful.

So to come to a place where I can admit I experienced trauma and needed healing feels like a big deal. To put it in a book so that other humans can read it is an even bigger deal. Wouldn't it be nice to be fully entertained by a book about something fun? I wish I were that girl! But it's time to stop wishing for that. It's time to fully get comfy with my humanity and also fully embrace God's unimaginable bigger-than-life love for me!

He is a happy God, in a good mood. He is ready for the fun! I believe with all my heart that He's here for the party. He loves a good idea and wants to put in the effort to pull off the surprise of a lifetime and give the best gift and laugh the hardest. He sees the depths of beauty in every soul. At every sunrise, He is saying, "Wake up! Wake up! It's your morning. This is your day. Let's go!" Yet He isn't single-faceted or short-sighted. He knows how to be in the hard spots with me. He doesn't shy away from sin or pain, hate or insecurity.

When I finally was willing to follow Him and handle the shadows of my life, only then could I really be myself. I met myself, really. Without the guard. Without the hiding. Full of life. Still plenty of layers to work through but so much braver than before. I was willing to push into the darkness with excitement and confidence about what was to come.

The funny thing is, I strived for years to be a girl who could write a book, but I had to go through a million moments of unraveling to learn that I didn't need to write a book to be a fully whole, loved daughter of God. I am perfectly held by him, enjoyed by him, loved by him. So now I can write a book, securely in my purpose as His daughter.

I always thought the right time would come to write a book. I won't even lie; I thought the skies would be clear and there would miraculously be an oceanfront house with a porch swing ready for writing (Nicholas Sparks style). Instead, I've written this book as my worship through weaning my very cuddly eighteen-month-old from breast-feeding, simultaneously detaching my prying fingers, one at a time, from my growing teenager all while trying to get my ten-year-old to just go to school.

Most of the writing came in spurts, at a red light or when I stole away to the toilet, or when I am supposed to be asleep during the middle of the night. Essentially, I am no one to anyone outside of the walls of my house, so there is no  pressure really for this book to meet some standard. The pressure comes more from creating a balance between continuing to be everything to the beautiful people in my house and this desire to serve you, friend, and that sweet and messy middle is a sacred space, where relying on a loving God is all that I have and I am settled in the fact that it is enough.

The telling of a fragile story is an invitation to soften the world through connection. Every chapter and every word is grueling, largely debated, all within my own head. I ask myself, *'Does this help? Does this hurt someone? How do I share the truth but honor each person in my story?*

No matter what role they played in this book, in my life, I do honor every person, and I am genuinely thankful for them and that role. I see each person through the lens of compassion, though it hasn't always been that way. Emotions are tricky like that: unreliable at best, but my tears can also be my guide toward curiosity, hunger for life, and the propensity for more, the abundant life we are designed to crave. All that to say, I very carefully chose what to include, making sure it only reflected my own perspective, in order to respect others, so please understand when some details are omitted.

There are things I'd love to do again because they're fun, but there are just as many things that have given me wish for a redo. I really wish I hadn't wasted seasons I spent worrying about this or that. I wish I could have known that it would work out. I wish I could have chosen better. I wish I would have chilled out and enjoyed the good pieces. All this wishing leaves me feeling as if I lost. Today I choose gratitude for every hard season, knowing that here I stand more beautiful than before.

I can't go back in time to make wishes come true, but God is gracious and took me as close as possible. We, me and God, weird I know, went on a trip back through my life to rewrite the narrative of my heart, essentially rewriting my future into the hope-filled one He promised. Even though I've always been skeptical that He had any unique promises for me, it turns out He's pretty invested in me. He's got my name on lock and all the details have already been anticipated, covered, and not only are they good, they are good for me. It's been a matter of seeing time as a gift. It gives and gives. Every hour, I can see beauty and gifts. This book is woven by a season of trips I took to visit old friends to tell my story. I will reference driving here and there on these trips. Grand things happen on the car rides and with the friends. I am just clarifying why I am always driving!

I wanted an adventure. I can honestly say this turned out to be a pretty good one.

Ironically, I think the plan for this book was in place long before I ever saw it coming. I spent a year teaching women who were taking a required parenting class. It was all about choosing life or death. I taught truths beyond my understanding long before I could apply them well. "Keep going. Keep practicing truth," I would tell them. "God will apply them to each layer as needed. The Bible is full of scriptures pointing us toward life. Make the choice to live. Make the choice to be courageous. Choose life. Speak life. Live!"

When God speaks, it creates life. Every time. It can't be helped. His voice, His presence makes new. Chains that bind your heart and limit your life break. So as you read the words of this book, there might come a desire to try to do something, emulate something I have done to get the same result. Say, "No," to that. Don't overthink; just be. Literally just come before the Father and be with Him! Over and over and over, practice believing His presence is with you and it is good. Just lay it out there, whatever is on your mind. Honest, raw, open. This response opens up space for good things to happen. I make space and trust Him with the rest. His word is 100% true. It will never fail. His purpose for you doesn't waver based on your actions. And absolutely do not compare your relationship with Him to mine. Choose today to believe He is for you.

I know a whole lot about internal dialogue. Mine goes something like this:

I feel dumb.
God says, "Enough digging. Enough talk. Time for action!"

I am inadequate.
God says, "It's time. In action, you will be proven what you need to know."

I don't know what to say.
God says, "When I speak, life forms."

I'm not the right person for the job.
God says, "Move forward in leadership. Share the truth."

I don't often connect the old wise leader of the Ten Commandments with the young, rebellious, confused, and overwhelmed runaway. Through the end of Moses' life, we can see a deepened softened intimacy between him and the Lord, an established trust because of the actions he took in response to meeting with God throughout his journey. I hope my journey gives similar outcomes, but with less drama would be just fine.

God's command is to "love the Lord your God with your whole heart", despite my feelings, in response to my feelings, and along with all my feelings. Loving him with my whole heart includes my creativity and ideas and enthusiasm, my fun and planning, my inclusive inviting. It's also with my brokenness, my fears, my worries, my inadequacies. It all works together to breathe life into the future. I love him and come to him in my humanity plus the covering of His grace. That is my whole heart.

As I surrender to God's presence and trust Him, I find rest there. Through this trip of going back in time to seek God, meeting him again on every page of my life, I've settled into a place of knowing that nothing can shake who we are together.

How can you see into my eyes like open doors?
Leading you down into my core where I've become so numb
Without a soul, my spirit's sleeping somewhere cold
Until you find it there and lead it back home
Wake me up inside
(I can't wake up) wake me up inside
(Save me) call my name and save me from the dark
(Wake me up) bid my blood to run
(I can't wake up) before I come undone
(Save me) save me from the nothing I've become
Now that I know what I'm without, you can't just leave me
Breathe into me and make me real
Bring me to life

Evanescence, Bring Me to Life

1

Wake Up!

Wake up, sleepy head! Rise and shine!

My kids will say they are awake, even look me in the face and answer a yes/no question, but they are for sure still very much asleep. They won't remember a single word they agreed to in those moments of swollen eyes that just refuse to open and arms still snuggled deeply under their warm bellies. Let's be honest, they can actually be fully awake and still claim complete ignorance of every word I've said! That being said, we can all agree our hearts absolutely swell with immense love for our kids when they are sleeping. Then they wake!

Sometimes things are easier when we walk in ignorant bliss, right? But is this really living? If we don't go for the more God offers, then what is left? What are we actually choosing when we sleep through an automatic, mundane life?

My mom would use the biggest threat of all, "When your dad gets home," only after I had pushed and pushed to a point of no return. She would be so exasperated with me and ready for some reinforcements with a little more power. Except this didn't really scare me much. I'm not saying I liked getting a spanking, from her or him, but it didn't change my behavior for very long. Maybe that power struggle made me feel alive, if even for a moment.

That fight for a feeling of control started early. We do all kinds of things to make us feel alive. That first sunburn of the summer. That fresh haircut. Don't even get me started on good brows! Nothing beats a new pair of blue jeans just right on the backside. A concert where you know every word. A chocolate layered cake with mousse and chocolate shavings and a moist bottom layer. Laughter with friends. Such good, good things.

We do all kinds of things to feel awake too! We make plans; we read the news; we donate and volunteer; we play hard and love with fierceness. Could it be, while we do all these things, we are just sleeping? Can we try our hardest and still feel robbed of time and full of regret at the end? If it was all suddenly over, what was the point of it all or would we have a confidence that we had known our gifts, used them fully, and lived a life poured out? Does this futile attempt to control, in reality, stifle our hard-sought freedom, preventing the flow of what has been designed specifically for our best? I have countless stories where I took over a plan and forced an outcome instead of trusting someone else to give me something generous or leaving space for someone to fill a need or even a fun desire in my life. My control, stemmed from fear of not having the best, robs me of a life full of treasures and beauty and surprises.

"I know all that you do, and I know that you have a reputation for being really "alive," but you're actually dead! Wake up and strengthen all that remains before it dies, for I have not found your works to be perfect in the sight of my God. So remember all the things you've received and heard, then turn back to God and obey them. For if you continue to slumber, I will come to you like a thief, and you'll have no idea at what hour I will come." Revelation 3:1-3.

I think God, here in Revelation 3, isn't threatening doom and gloom. Rather, it's like when you're at Disney and it's the end of the night and you know the fireworks are happening but you also want to be in the shortest line for the ride so you can hop back on several times. I did this in high school with my girl, Andrea. We must have ridden Space Mountain five times before sprinting to the bus, where every sleepy face glared at us because they'd been waiting a little too long past curfew. These two goody goodies just had to squeeze every allowable ounce of fun from that park and I'm not sure how anyone could blame us! Honestly, I blame them for not joining in. I'm always one for including as many as possible in all the fun and don't want anyone to miss out, no matter that their idea of fun could differ from mine.

I repeated this exact pattern when we took our boys to Disney many years later. We watched the fireworks but also positioned ourselves to take a couple trips on Big Thunder Mountain in the dark and snag a foot-long hotdog on the way out. Who wants to waste time on the food?! Who am I kidding? I plan all things around what good food is available!

It doesn't matter where we go, I am going to pack in plans for every single minute and have it mapped out on Google Maps to optimize each ounce of energy that I'm usually trying to pull from my boys. I am pretty sure it's a love-hate relationship they have with me, the way I push for immense fun. I'm curious how that will transition in their adulthood. I'm not really sorry. I think I know fun best and once I drag them in, they usually agree. Except maybe that backpacking trip when we each carried thirty plus pounds and by mile ten it wasn't so fun because we struggled to find somewhere to pitch our tent. Sorry, boys.

This urgency to live your life is that fifteen-minute warning that, "TJMaxx will be closing soon. Make your selections!" It's saying, "Hey, don't forget what you love. Don't get distracted with all the fluffy stuff allowing the real things of life to pass by."

What is it that you really want? What do you crave from life or from your spouse or from your friends? What does God have that you want?

They say time flies when you're having fun, but give me a survey and I'm going to bubble in 'strongly disagree'. Having fun is knowing what you've done and where you are going and feeling satisfied with those choices. My biggest pet peeve is time flying out of my control and me not having a clue if I did my best with it. Was I where I was supposed to be? Did I miss what God had for me then?

It's taken some serious work, and let's be honest, I'm still slap in the middle of learning to believe that I am where I am meant to be and that God is for me here and now. He is here now. I am good here now. Life is sweet here now. I do not need to worry about what I'm missing or that I won't know where to go or when to be there.

Learning to be human has played a huge role in this development. But equally, it has impressed on me the desire to keep living. Instead of living in fear, living awake! Full of life! Through this transition I started to ask some questions:

What is it that gives me life? What is *not* for me?

Take time to notice. Pay attention—to red flags; to curiosity.

Is there space to listen? To be creative? Is there time to just be?

Before, I didn't think so.

Presence is over everything else. Presence gives clarity. Presence fulfills, satisfies.

Jesus knew the importance of presence and lived it every day.

One synoptic account says large crowds were wild as Jesus entered Jerusalem. Spoiler alert! He had just resurrected a man from the dead. Hello, even in Bible times, that wasn't normal! So this mystery guy gets to the city basically via parade. I'm just picturing that time our family watched the Disney parade from the treehouse on Tom Sawyer's Island. I'm just saying, we might not be VIP, but we were watching that parade like Peter Pan's lost boys that day: wild and full of wonder up in the trees. The best view and full of delight. We knew we had the most magical seats in the park!

I'm actually not obsessed with Disney, but it gives good illustrations.

They watched Jesus with delight that day too! They scrambled around finding the best spot to see the one who could change everything. Full of hope and cries filled with anticipation of something new, something more than the arrival of Ariel and Cinderella on their floats. They were hoping for an important change that they had needed for a long time. I wonder if they even knew what they wanted.

Jesus asks that so often. "What do you want?" As if he has insight that life is fleeting. It can definitely give a person pause. They are just scrambling to the front for something better not even knowing what that could be. A resurrection of any kind. A desperation for meaning. Maybe even if our minds don't know, our spirits know that we need the one who gives life, creates it even. Our souls cry out for more, something higher, something we can't grasp or see. We don't even know what we want, so we grab at every passing thing hoping it will cure our thirst for value, for real life.

So many of us have been hoping he'd see us, hoping he'd hear that cry for help, answer that prayer, even if it was only thrown around in our head like a whisper to the stars, just hoping it lands somewhere helpful. When will he listen? Does he even hear me? But it's year after year of the same. Dejected. we decide it's up to our own effort to make this life the best it can be.

So Jesus gets to the city and the gospel of Luke reads he wept for Jerusalem. Just overwhelmed with grief, their suffering and the suffering bound to come. He swipes the temple of greed, restoring its purity. God creates best in vast spaces. We don't necessarily know the order of these events but we do know that he left Jerusalem for Bethany and I want to know why.

We know Jesus has a habit of finding alone time. This isn't because he is an introvert or any other label that risks to confine. I imagine it is because when he abided with his Father, he was clear on identity and mission. Plain and simple. Less distraction, less exhaustion. Full of awakened life.

I know when I get in a crowd of people, I start listening to the crowd, what they want, what they don't like, what they expect. Whatever the order of events that day in Jerusalem, I feel sure he felt a range of strong emotions. Talk about the trip of a lifetime. This is when everything changes. He knows peace is soon to be theirs but I'm sure "peace" isn't what the crowds were shouting. Changed hearts wasn't the demand that day, so coming back to quiet must have been very intentional and a model to us on how to live that one life fully awake, fully engaged with an in-the-zone viewpoint. Aligning, providing, clarifying for his mission, this time opened a direct line, from God to him and him alone. He didn't go to social media or the latest podcast for a sign. He needed to know exactly what God was saying so he could get this right without people pleasing, without exhaustion, just clear-minded and set on a path that is true.

The connection directly to Heaven is the only true path to the awakened life that your soul craves. It does crave it, doesn't it? Is that just me? I feel that way so often. I stop typing and run to TJMaxx or binge a show because it seems like that is what everyone is doing and they're all so happy, plus facing the truer reality can be hard and lonely. I don't walk around seeing people hurting and longing for Spirit life, the hidden cravings of our souls. This fear that I am alone in this hunger shuts me down, but God wakes me back up, 'rise and shine sleeping beauty,' and I press on with this offering of making "the more" possible. Front row in the parade. The best view is ours. The connection to the Creator, the one who breathes new life, is ours. It's available!

You have all my attention
I will linger and listen
I can't miss a thing
Lord, I know my heart wants more of You
My heart wants something new
So I surrender it all
All I want is to live within Your love
Be undone by who You are
My desire is to know You deeper
Lord I will open up again
Throw my fears into the wind
I am desperate for a touch of heaven

Hillsong Worship, Touch of Heaven

2

Belonging

I was driving when He said *stop*.

My chest was starting to constrict with tension. This difficulty breathing was becoming more and more familiar. "No thanks. I'll just pass on through this and keep going."

There is no condemnation here. Please stop.

I had no idea what I had started when I made the impulsive decision to drive down for one night to a town that had stripped me of everything I was, but God knew and orchestrated every detail. Like the piles of rubbish on every corner of this city, He would take each piece of what I saw as trash and rebuild my life. I didn't really know God quite like this before this happened. Everything that happened was completely new and unique to this season.

This book is my heart wrenched open and mended in a million ways. Every thread stitched with precision, piercing pain and pulling through to freedom. So so many cries of "no thanks, not that detail, they don't want to read that. Don't make me say it. What even is the point?" I tried to create a formula, make it doable and fail-proof. I wanted to promise you, my reader and therefore trusted friend, a result. I wanted to be impressive. I wanted to make God accessible. I wanted to put him in a tube and squeeze Him on a page and give Him a 1-2-3. "In 1-2-3 you too can have God's voice!" Like he is a genie in a bottle. I can hear Will Smith's Genie voice, from Aladdin, echoing in my room, "What can I do for you?!"

Truth is He is easy to find. I do want to promise it! His voice is available. I feel confident! He speaks and calls every person. He gives purpose. I believe these things all the time... most of the time... okay, some of the time. I also hear the objections of: "How is this even possible?"

I know the doubts closely. Is there even someone up there listening? I understand the circumstances where it doesn't feel that way or it didn't work out or He didn't save me or prevent that thing from happening. I felt that way when I was on the bathroom floor vomiting daily from stress, feeling completely alone in the world. I've been in that place where I have asked God for help but got no response.

So finally I conceded that there is no formula. If there was, I'd probably charge a lot more and have a personal jet. Headliner: Small town girl with no Instagram following finds direct access to God of the universe!

Actually, I have found God, as many have, but there is no formula. When I was spilling my guts about this, I was asked, well what worked for you? Did an Instagram post getcha? Did a book you read help? Nope, no, nah none of that. Sure, I get encouragement from something, a little boost and challenge here or there.

So what worked? Literally only the voice of God becoming real and true for ME; a direct line from Him to me. His voice for someone else? Powerless. His voice in a sermon? It's ok, but I usually forget by the time my pizza rolls are sizzling in the oven.

When I knew for sure that God was real and He was constantly inspiring me, speaking to me, leading me, using my creativity, a world that seemed to be spinning out of control came into a settled rotation of order and meaning. No longer was comparison a thief. No longer did I worry that I wasn't doing the right thing enough to make Him speak to me. He wasn't withholding. He wasn't angry. He hadn't moved on to someone cooler, prettier, smarter. I had heard the voice and now I was different. I was chosen. It became, well, easy.

After He asked me to stop, I drove a little farther down the bay front road. I thought I was taking the scenic route for fun, just to drool longingly over gorgeous historic brick homes with pristine yards shaded by mature oaks. These aren't cookie-cutter giant square houses shoved into a cul-de-sac for grand effect. These are snuggled in as if they were here first. They set the standard for belonging and everyone around knows it. They don't even have to try, they are just cool, lofty with imperfections, I might add, since I'm dissecting my love relationship with old houses. I marvel at the cozy combination of timeless homes against a view of white sand and still clear waters. Is everything in my life I long for found in places of belonging? It must be what I'm drawn to.

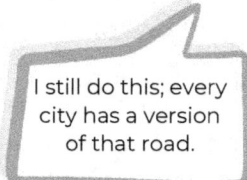
I still do this; every city has a version of that road.

Naturally, a space for parking came into view, so I obediently, though uncertain; reluctantly, though curious, parked the car that day. I didn't have to walk far and not a soul was in sight. I didn't have a clue what I was supposed to be doing. Do I walk? Do I stay still? So I just sat awkwardly on a log at the bay's shore. Oddly out of place, yet peacefully protected amidst trees. It really is such a unique place. It felt like the world I had wanted mixed with the grief of falling short, unreaching. A place of imperfect coolness but instead of looking like aged beauty, my imperfections more resembled the piles of trash left by the recent hurricane.

Unexpected peace filled my heart right there in that spot. Undeserved to say the least, but soothing, like cold lotion after a day in the windy beach sun. The words of the Father spoke, *there is no condemnation here,* and in that moment, I believed them. There weren't any tears. I didn't lift my hands. I barely prayed except initially to say, "No thanks." I didn't say much. Honestly, in that instant, I didn't have a major event I was unlocking or trying to understand. I had not arrived with an expectation or need from God. He found me. It started with feelings of shame cloaking me in regret that only showed up in my shallow breathing. After that gentle touch it was gone because I stopped and He met me there. I believed Him.

"I wonder who can see through my mask of efforts. I don't understand why I'm not happy. I have everything to be satisfied and yet I can't."

When I wrote these thoughts in 2012, I was so completely discontent. I was disappointed in so many things: my life, my dirty floors, my marriage. Everything bothered me at once. These symptoms are not ones to be ignored. We can and should explore what is causing them. Interestingly, I think I was happy, pretty happy, or at least I remember it happily. I wouldn't know I felt otherwise if I hadn't read it right out of my own handwriting. Also, noted, we can feel completely happy and full of gratitude and simultaneously be carrying heavy burdens. We are complex people and that is okay. I don't mean to sound despondent, but these are the deepest pieces of who I was and am, so they don't necessarily cover the day-to-day fun and joy with family and activities and kids, but know that those things were happening successfully.

These writings are the nuances of the whole person and I think that deeper inspection of self allows recognition that, even in our beautiful lives, our substance is layered in many many rays of emotion and longings, as well as gratitudes and choices to enjoy the life we have and the moments we are in. Nonetheless, this particular memoir is one of a deeper search and so I started year thirty-three asking for a renewal. Renew the joy of my salvation. And I started to ask this question, "Could my calling, my beauty, be just to be me?" I wrote in that year's journal:

> Maybe success for a female is
> just seeing her own beauty.

I went on to write of soaking in every morsel of God I could find, usually via other's experiences, and spent the whole time wishing it was me. Wishing I was them. Wishing I was Godly enough. Trying to absorb Godliness.

Reading the journal from 2015 broke my heart for my younger self. How do I reconcile all of this grief? A grief she was not even aware of. She is so lost and so hungry for truth. Yet she had it. She knew the Lord and loved Him deeply, but she absolutely didn't know His love for her. The yearning continued to be documented on every page, *"But I'm not Godly - not like that. Not like the one who always has the words. Not like the one who is quick to serve. Not like the one who knows exactly how to give Jesus glory in every Facebook post. You know her, she's beautiful. Where is my beauty? Maybe it's not in trying to be like her."*

> She knew the Lord and loved Him dearly, but she absolutely didn't know His love for her.

Journals are angsty that way, full of mostly your moments of needing to vent. I have a journal from high school and let me tell you, slap full of teenage angst. "Hey God - How is Heaven? Earth is..earth. I guess." Constantly asking dumb things, "What is your will? I want to do what's right. What do you want? I'm screaming inside." I mean, girl, just make a decision about how you want to spend Spring Break and go with it! Geez, drama!

"My mom and I do not even get along. She makes all these rules. 'Just because,' is what she says. 'Whatever,' is what I say."

When I was not asking God about a guy I was making a list.

1. Quiet time
2. Get dressed - do not be lazy
3. Homework - just do your best!
4. Wednesdays - time with Tyler
5. Drink water

How did I have "drink water" on my to do list for thirty years and I still don't drink water? These are the deepest questions of life.

There are pages where I was excited about our new sister coming from China! She brought all the joy! And there are prayers of petition for God's will on my science test. Naturally, every entry is signed, "a+f", always and forever, with a heart and a flower, a smiley face, and a Jesus fish. Or simply "I'm audi".

Thankfully, my journals, then or now, don't encapsulate all my feelings. My life was slam packed with all the happy things that I loved, as a teen, but also as a fully grown-up woman, wife, and mom. I chose the things that kept me busy, and I felt intentional about them. I believed not just that being busy was important, but that keeping myself busy made me important, that it gave me purpose. So much so that, when I tried to come up with my purpose, my one thing, I felt torn between all the amazing things in my life that I couldn't let go of. This sounds like I mean at age seventeen when I was trying to determine my path. No, this is in my thirties when I am still trying to determine my path! I see now that these things were idols to me, all in place to give me identity. I described my life like driving a car too fast. But when I slam on brakes, instead of stopping, my car rolls bumpily over my brakes. While in one moment, I was already planning the next; never fully present. I didn't notice the sweet things of now.

I loved now and felt positive about it, but always had my foot moving to the next thing. No matter my efforts, my eyes always saw bigger plans and new ideas. I was not wishing things away in the now, I enjoyed life, but not without distraction and confusion about what was mine to do.

Continuing to reflect about how to slow down and reduce my busyness, two pages after I was seeking out my "one major thing". I was journaling the age-old question, "When will God let me teach? When will I get to share my writing?" I was completely oblivious to my own heart as well as my own self-sabotage. Oblivious to how my to-dos were dictating my life. There was zero space for me to minister to the Lord and be useful to create true life.

In writing this memoir, I read at least twenty journals and every one referenced writing a book! But then, I was looking for more things "to do". God was just waiting on me to do what my heart was longing for. He was ready and willing to help! He did eventually navigate through all of it and invite me into this time and space and cleared the stage so I could do what I love. He gave me permission to worship Him with my oil. To pour it out in a way that honored Him, but also honored me, although writing feels a waste at times, especially when the floors need mopping.

My purpose alone is to prepare a way for God. To know Him and be known. May His favor go before you and behind you, all around you as you read my story. May His voice resound as you discover your identity in a deeper way and may your voice find its place, full of awakened life.

I used to be mean
Couldn't care 'bout a thing
Living for me
And all of my needs
I was self serving
Yet desperate and hurting
In need to be
Not the same
No, no, no, yeah, yeah, yeah
Jesus has changed me
Not the same

Crystal Lewis, Not the Same

3
Good Girl vs. Bad Girl

My legs were surrounded by green slimy arms of seaweed trying to pull me under. Voices everywhere above me were yelling for me to swim. There was no reason I should not have been able to swim. I had experience swimming aptly on a swim team, but I simply could not propel my body to move. I was flailing and frozen at the same time. In my mind I was already dead! Chomped up into a million pieces. My dad eventually dove into the very small space between the paddle boats for my grand rescue.

It didn't feel like I would need to be rescued. It felt like I should have known how to get out. Just reach out my arm and climb back to safety. But I didn't know how. I couldn't think. I couldn't swim. I couldn't process all the voices or even ask for help. The only way was to be rescued.

As our friends and family paddled meekly, as if with tails tucked between their legs, back to shore, the park ranger was wildly blowing his whistle and shouting through a megaphone that gave him immense authority as if he knew something we didn't. He was yelling, "NO SWIMMING!" because the lake was well known to be slap full of alligators. I'm sure he was wondering why on earth anyone would jump in! Of course, he didn't know that I had fallen in by accident during our game of throwing soggy bread at each other.

Much the same could be said about my life. They must all be saying, "Why on earth did she jump in?"

Honesty is not something I ever lacked as a little girl. My whole family laughs in a common understanding that "Riley tells it like she sees it". Apparently, I didn't have the knack yet for stating things in a way that helps more than hurts; not saying anything at all didn't seem like an option. You knew exactly what I thought at all times.

I got it from my great grandma, Pete, affectionately named by her daddy. We just added a good southern Mama to the front and to us she was Mama Pete. She also had a knack with using her voice and saying the darndest things. My own sweet mama is still very much living so I better be careful but let's just say, it runs in the family. Effectively whispering or saying something just for the sake of making someone else look better isn't usually our default. We tend to blunt-like blurt and maybe later apologize.

We threw Mama Pete a surprise 90th birthday party. My sister-in-law and I thought for sure we needed to stand behind her as she entered the room in case she fell out from shock. Needless to say, that was not a problem. The maturing woman who still sat with her long leg with knee bent, foot in the chair, her arm casually wrapped around it, entered that party and owned it, yelling, "It's a party!" With flair, she threw her gangly arms from a 6-foot body in the air and had the time of her life.

All my life she wore big rings on as many fingers as would fit, and even more bracelets! On top of her head, she wore big bright red curls, similar to Bozo the clown, but she wore it better. Much better; plus her personality called for big hair. She had been "doing hair" in her in-home shop for longer than I had been alive in a tiny town where both of my parents grew up. I still have  That was a TV show in the 80s. the occasional patient at work who knew her from yard hoppin'. She could survey a yard sale in seconds to know if there were any treasures there. I'll take a comparison to her flamboyant character any time, usually given by my husband, and wear it proudly. You can find lots of stories about her, because, of course, she has her very own hashtag: #formamapetessake.

I think when I was born, all my grandmothers and greats got said roles at too young an age and weren't ready for the full commitment to the elderly titles, so I have a Mama Pete, Mary, Jerry, Mama Graham, Granny B and Jimmy. I do also have Poppa and my favorite Nana and I do so cherish each of them and their names. Endearing or plain, makes no difference to me.

Every time I call my Granny B, my grandmother on my dad's side, she answers the phone, "Hey Riley Jane." I think Jane has a reputation for being a plain name. Coming from my Granny's lips gives it an air of elegance and love; however, I am, in fact, very plain. I don't know how not to say things exactly as I think them. It's obnoxious and aggravating. I don't know how to say things in a good way. I don't say things that draw people in or make them want to tell me things. I may be guarded but it's usually just to keep from looking dumb. If you ask me anything, I just tell every detail, plainly, exactly as it is. I know no other way. It just comes out. I watch other people and they omit so many details and I wonder why I didn't think of that. They have mystery. Also, if I'm super honest, that detail that I wish I had some of in my life really annoys me, because I'd much prefer to fully know the person I'm friends with without all the mystery, especially since it's almost a guarantee they know all of me, if they give me any quality time at all.

Whatever I was doing as a child, I was doing it with full enthusiasm. 100 percent all the time, never time for the dull or mundane. I wanted life to be grand. Sincere and inclusive.

Somehow despite my lack of couth, Granny B agreed to the start of the grandest of traditions: the Granny B and Riley Christmas Party. You had to say it like that every time. That was its formal name which it demanded because the attire was also formal. We made invitations and planned extravagant food, complemented by Rice Krispies treats, and had everyone bring a talent to perform. My grandpa Jimmy's tradition and talent was always to fondly read *The Night Before Christmas*, but Mama Pete changed hers up each year.

One year, she came dressed in a 20s flapper dress and performed the Charleston. One year, my parents brought an entire life-size game of Jeopardy. No matter what, the night could not end without us singing "The 12 Days of Christmas" in its entirety, charade style, with each number assigned to a few people who would stand and gesture each time their number came around. It was atrocious and my favorite thing of all time. Granny B had the right dishes for all occasions and more Christmas trees in her house than one can imagine. I grew up with one Christmas tree, hung with colored lights and all our mismatched family ornaments, but decorating it was just as much a treasured tradition as Christmas morning. Christmas was magical growing up!

Granny B always tells stories of me and laughs at how she always knew what I was thinking. As she tells these stories, her hand is always on my arm, tickling lightly with her polished fingernails. We always had a close relationship, but she only knew what I was thinking because I made it known very plainly.

She loves this one: "Riley asked me in the dressing room that day what all that stuff was on my back. I told her it was fat, just plain fat." I was just asking an honest question. I wouldn't know for a long time what plain fat even meant, but once it hit me I knew fully well because my body and Granny B's are very much the same.

Even though I was loud about some things, somehow I became silent when it came to anything important or personal. Somewhere in the years of planning parties with Granny, I grew older and just failed to share with my mom that I had started my cycle. It just never came up. I was private to a fault. Maybe this is where my pride began. My 'I can handle it by myself' mentality. I only ever presented myself as capable and independent, having no need.

It turns out all my rescues have been the silent kind. I didn't really know how to bring up the awkward ways of asking for help and letting one know that I had a need. My mom basically had to read my mind and she's been pretty good at that for a long time. I never really wanted her input, but I always loved having her near. She tells me I'd ask her to come play with me but I really just wanted her to sit in my room with me. Why am I so weird? Despite my lack of ability to be vulnerable or communicate, I guess my mom learned me because she knows when I need rescuing and tells me it's okay to need it.

I can still smell the mixture of gas and oil from the motorcycles in our garage. It could have been the Harley my dad was working on, but more than likely it was a Yamaha dirt bike, with a sticker on the front and the side, Number 107. We spent many many days at the races and anytime I get a whiff of it now, my heart melts in nostalgia. My dad and my brother, Tyler, would put on the thick pants and walk with the hard boots that made them take clunky steps. They wouldn't do their hair but would look cool anyways. We had the trailer set up and you just plopped right in the dirt, because there was no point in avoiding it. My freckled face would be bright red when I got hot from playing hard. It still does sometimes and I hate that, but my dad says he loves it. I love the smell of oil. It fills my chest with comfort, feels like home. At home I would just sit silently with my dad while he worked in the garage. I would just be nearby in case he needed me to hand him a wrench or if he dropped a screw and I could grab it. Sometimes I'd bring him a glass of sweet tea. "Thanks baby," he'd say. Not much for many words, an expert at one-liners, but I didn't care at all. I was so happy to just be near him and be together. I think it was mutual. There was plenty of space.

How much space would I need later in life to achieve the fully awakened life I longed for, though silence and introspection often won this fight? Would it take a full dunking to wash away the need to hide who I am? I would need several dunks to wake me from the numbness that comes with a pride cut so deep.

Even though I had started my relationship with God with a quiet whispered yes while using my practiced cheer clap on the front row of church, no one really even knew much. We didn't walk to the front or anything in our kind of church. I guess my mom knew somehow. I can't really remember, but I do know she always said I was so mean before I knew Jesus, and after that I was much easier

surely, she meant honest...

to be around! Whatever that means. I'm just kidding. I know exactly what it means. This girl has got some attitude!

It was a few years later before I decided to be baptized in front of my church in a new city (we moved every 3 years). All my youth group friends were sitting on the front row, and it felt really important and like I was choosing something that would change everything. It definitely felt like an entrance into something inclusive and I had always wanted to be included. Like everyone there who had done it before knew something I needed to know and I wanted to know too! Don't leave me behind! I'm doing it too! I belong here. I wish that water washing over me could have also washed away every confused thought and fear. I wished it could answer and erase anything that wasn't for me and rinse me in a bold identity. Just like I stepped into the baptismal pool that day, I would have to step into the identity that was fully mine.

All my life, I dreamed of being the beautiful bride and having all the beautiful babies. My favorite Barbies were wedding Barbie and Ken, with the twin babies and their strollers. I mostly spent my time decorating the house and fixing the furniture. I would take my dolls and stuffed animals and create clothes for them and cover them in makeup, which was usually glitter. I was always decorating homes for them in cardboard boxes, then gifting them to my mom because of course she would want them. Always dressing up and fixing, making them better. Creative and fun and ambitious. With barely a blink, make-believe with dolls phased into real life make believe. It wasn't until years later that I could see my life wasn't supposed to be lived as make-believe. I was still just playing dress up. I jumped in fully, not knowing into what.

With an early engagement, during college, we bought a four-poster bed from a printed flyer on the bus stop wall. You just tore off the phone number to call and buy the furniture. This was before Facebook Marketplace. It felt so fancy and grown up and too good to be true. My mom and I planned a dream wedding and decorated

my mom thrives in perfecting details!

everything to perfection: pink roses, a grand staircase, and a white dress with delicate details that would knock you off your feet. Since all the details were so perfect, I never stopped to wonder what the event planner meant when she confided in my mom that she didn't recognize me as the girl who'd visited, dewy-eyed, months before. When did make-believe start to lose its grandeur? It would only take a few short months for the dew to dry but years to understand that pulling away in the Rolls Royce was just the start of my facade.

That love, as sincere as I was at nineteen, really was created more from a place of fancy imagination. Regardless of the depth of love, the pain was very much real and lasting, leaving a gaping wound that would prevent me from rebuilding my life with depth or authenticity.

How could I have known that falling in young love and blindly following my dream life could end as quickly as it had begun in devastation, leaving me in a place full of judgment, rejection, and suddenly not belonging in the church that had become home?

I think I was born wanting to be a grown up. From the beginning I was always trying to be bigger. Fully grown, I barely reach a whole five feet, so all my life I've been a head smaller than all my friends. They didn't even sell clothes to fit my body to match my age. My mom was so patient and generous to go to every story and try every option to find the most grown up things in the little girls' department, even into high school. I've always wanted to make a place for myself, show up, be visible. I had never really gained a lot of attention from the male population. Well maybe that isn't true. I had little boyfriends here and there. I'm pretty sure I still have one from the four months we lived in Illinois. Sorry Ian Fischer. I said no to the guy who asked me, a sophomore, to his senior prom. I do not even know his name now. I said no because I was terrified he would try to kiss me! We met while I was learning the dances for the school pageant. It was a Hawaiian theme. The costume was a simple shirt with a teeny floral wrap skirt. I was never very popular but friendly enough with everyone, as a cheerleader and all. The mom of the most popular girl in school said she was worried because she thought I might beat her daughter! That felt like a win enough to me to have given the popular girl's mom a scare! My dress had big boobs sewn into the top because there wouldn't be any otherwise. My mom curled my hair, stacking it big on top, probably to make me a little taller. I couldn't have weighed more than 75 lbs.

I genuinely don't know if I should paint my character as the good girl or the bad girl. Is both an option? I didn't mean to be a bad girl. That was definitely never my plan and I honest to goodness wouldn't even say I chose it. It feels more like it chose me, jumped on me really. I wanted to be good, but I kept being bad, no matter how bad I wanted to be good! I didn't set out to be bad when we moved to a completely new town in the middle of my junior year of high school. I wasn't tempted by normal things. I never even attended a party to experience any peer pressure. All my friends were very—well, no matter what I say, it feels incomplete or stereotypical or something—Christian, wholesome, moral. Is that what makes a girl good? Because wasn't I that too? And, quite frankly, aren't girls who aren't Christian also good? Indeed, they are.

My idea of fun was the church lock-in where we played sardines in the church bells. I wanted to watch Clueless at the slumber party where the worst thing we did was freeze someone's bra if she dared go to sleep first. Sure there was that time I was asked to smoke in the back of the school, but I had already had enough second-hand cigarette smoke in my life and didn't want a thing to do with it. Things have a way of sneaking in the back though. I remember when my best friend in middle school started meeting boys at the movies to kiss. I was so behind, but eventually I caught up plenty. One person's temptation is another's ease, but fear not being left out, everyone has something. I found mine, dressed it up, and called it love.

I definitely had plenty of opportunities after that for experience. I was still a church girl. I sang soprano in the band at our new church. Even got up early for the sunrise Easter service in the park. I led kids on a Friday night outreach team. I volunteered at a women's shelter tutoring children.

It's all so duplicitous. Not intentionally, but nonetheless. In case there is any confusion, the sinner and the saint are the same person. I suppose calling myself the worst of sinners is a bit dramatic and of course it is all relative to whom you're around, but like I said, my friends were saints.

What worked with my dad just wasn't cutting it this time. I would sit in our first apartment, in a hand-me-down armchair, covered in dark velvety flowers for hours, just to be present. '*Maybe if I sit long enough and be the right person and look pretty I can be enough.*'

The months grew more and more silent and a glass of tea didn't do the trick. The love that started out didn't feel like love anymore. My days became numb, grasping for what is right, what is good. I had no place to belong. I tried to put in place all the things I saw my parents do. I separated from friends and chose a church *just for us*. I worked really hard, paying for a full-time college load with cash. I did everything I could to make him proud, but it wasn't enough. I became invisible and I felt completely alone. Where was my happy ending? Why didn't anyone fight for me? Why was everything I did not enough?

There are some seasons that are so black it feels beauty is impossible to find, though I am certain it is there. The blackness feels like it will swallow you whole, never letting you get back to the life you were trying to create. I got sick one time while living in Orlando. So sick that I was in bed for days and when I woke, I had no memory of the days that had passed. I only know because my coworkers had placed balloons in my room and told me so after.

At the start of the illness, I had tried to host a women's church event in my apartment. We had the Target version of couch slipcovers and a lamp my brother had given me set on the floating shelves, of course, all inspired by Pottery Barn. Tyler, my brother, who was still in high school at the time, was offended that the lamp was in my living room and told my mom that if I valued it at all, I would have it in my bedroom. I guess that makes sense for a teenager. What did I do? Of course, I moved it to my bedroom. I had to send all the women home early from that event. My lungs hurt so badly I was sure I wouldn't make it and that all my ribs must be broken. I exaggerate not. It's hard for me to remember or pull any value from the season that started then and lasted three years. Grief and deep sorrow consumed me like my aching ribs. I was broken beyond repair. Toward the end, I slid down the wall drunk for the first time, but was left alone again. Apparently being drunk didn't make me any more appealing.

When I knew it was over, my daddy came to my rescue, again. No questions asked, but full of compassion. Just drove down, got my stuff, drove home, and gave me my room back, kind of. I had never lived in that house specifically. My parents had moved "home" at the time of my dad's retirement from the USAF, but I chose the independent, brazen choice to move nine hours in the opposite direction to college. It's ingrained in me to choose the harder thing. My dad's only advice was a last-minute comment right before they drove away after moving me into my college apartment, "Don't pretend to be married." I guess he already knew that I was good at make-believe.

I heartily committed as if I lived in a fairy tale and everything would work itself out in my favor. I thought my relationship would parallel my parents' hard-earned love story. I thought a good love story had to be fought for. At that age, even though I had heard how hard they fought, all I knew was their love for me and their fight for one another and it just felt like a romance novel with all the good parts of hard and fight and conquering. I thought that must be what it was supposed to be, a dirty t-shirt you can never take off. It never occurred to me I could follow a different path and choose something easier, God-given, centered, and full of life. The one-liner given when I got home was a Proverb (26:11): a dog returns to his vomit. No matter how many chances I was given, I always chose my own way over God's wisdom, but this time, I would not be going back. This was the end of that marriage and the start of a second chance.

After this my heart was tempted to quit, run away and hide, be numb, rebel. I needed rescuing! Unlike the rushing water of baptism over my face, or the lake experience where my dad was there and jumped in, this drowning felt inescapable, like I would never come up for air. Like no one would ever see me again. Everything I wanted was gone. /was gone. Failure as my reality set in like a cloak burying me beneath, but I didn't take time to acknowledge it.

When being the good girl I was meant to be didn't happen, I filled my days with so much good I couldn't breathe. Busyness and fun became my mantra. I did them like a pro! That didn't change the reality that who I am is one who goes astray. I fall and fail and deny like Peter. I sink like him too!

Then God drew me into a place of space, where He can make new things. From there He could heal my heart by taking me on a journey.

Clear the stage and set the sound and lights ablaze
If that's the measure you must take to crush the idols
Jerk the pews and all the decorations too
Until the congregations few then have revival
Tell your friends that this is where the party ends
Until you're broken for your sins, you can't be social
Then seek the Lord and wait for what He has in store
And know that great is your reward so just be hopeful
Cause you can sing all you want to
Yes you can sing all you want to
You can sing all you want to and still get it wrong,
Worship is more than a song

Jimmy Needham, Clear the Stage

4
Grand Plans

I have spent mounds of time and energy seeking God all over the place, mostly all over Instagram, Facebook, in other people's books, sermons, etc. I did my very best to get it right and do good, like I think most of us do. Somehow I don't feel like that intention of God's best lines up with this exhausting feeling of max effort to just make it to Friday every week. We're burnt out and wishing for an escape. We can't fix our spouses or our children. We can't live our dream life. We're just kind of stuck here in normal land doing normal things. Every now and then we set a big goal and thrust our effort into achieving it for a feeling of accomplishment but then it goes back to normal. I'm always falling into normal. The lavish grace of Jesus is that He invites us, pursues and calls us into a space where we can live for more. He makes Himself available in a really dynamic way that has nothing to do with church or sermons or following influencers. It's the most personal way possible. It's in you. I didn't know that when all this began, or maybe I knew the line, but had no idea the depths of its impact.

Story story story. I really don't know why the obsession with stories. Jesus must love them because he taught in stories all the time, to the point of frustration for his listeners and I dare say for some readers today—insert raised hand! I think the indirectness of them allows us to connect and resonate, to be able to see ourselves, when otherwise we can't seem to see ourselves accurately at all. I guess I could say I felt called to storytelling. I don't know... I had a moment with God at church camp. Most of my memories don't last, but there are a few that never fade. It wasn't a big deal at the time, but it just kind of stuck in my head until now. Actually I wanted to tell my story with speaking and song and I'm not really sure what I thought I was going to say. Did

> I literally never thought about either of these.

I think I was going to talk about my favorite pizza or maybe about all my grand plans? I'm really not sure. Maybe I thought I'd invent a miracle serum or a cure for something! Could I open a school for cool kids and then we could talk about that?

Truth is I'm a terrible storyteller. If I try to tell a joke, it falls flat, very very flat. No one laughs. I think I must miss the whole point. Come to think of it, if someone is going to tell me a joke, it's best if I know in advance that I'm supposed to laugh because I get distracted trying to figure out the details and worry about someone's feelings or whatever and completely miss the joke. It's dreadfully awful. Almost worse than the fact that I can't remember lyrics to songs but singing and dancing is my favorite thing. So embarrassing. Whether *the moment* felt grand or not, something changed, because my priorities shifted that summer after camp. When I came home, I spent many nights on my bed poring over my Bible dreaming of being a Bible study teacher and writer. From that point on, that thought was deeply embedded in my mind and it felt like story had always been a part of me.

I took piano lessons as an adult in preparation for imaginary life. Of course, all dreams start that way and I am a believer that our prep puts us in a position to be ready to say yes to whatever God has for us. At my recital I was the oldest by ten years. I didn't have any parents in the audience but easily won the award for best dressed. I was in a dress from The Limited. It was linen with a rich brown v-neck on top that penciled into a straight skirt to my knees in white. It was lined with a silky slip that made it feel expensive and gorgeous. I wore it again a few years later when I graduated with my masters, ironically, not in writing, ministry, or theology, something that could have actually been helpful in dream life. Even then, God is so gracious and my job has in fact prepared me deeply for storytelling, because every patient tells one. Every patient is a podcast interview practice. Isn't that so funny? I spent my whole life living my life with the stage in mind. Anytime something would happen, I'd imagine myself on stage telling that part of the story, making people laugh, and what song I would sing with it! Well, if playing keys to The Little Mermaid is still on my agenda it will have to be at Level 2

> Isn't that the most obnoxious thing you've ever heard? But it's true!

preschool stage, because that's as far as I got in my lessons. Silly to think of me, twenty-two, in that fancy dress playing "Yankee Doodle Dandy". And I think I'm not courageous.

Also silly, I fully planned on traveling to orphanages around the world, giving my life in missions, having lots of children, having a city view window from a skyscraper with a house full of Pottery Barn monogrammed bedding. I was going to wear business attire like a lawyer on Suits and be a stay-at-home mom. I was going to lead worship and teach Bible studies. And, naturally, my hottie husband would adore me, all with Rachel hair and a flawless face provided by Mary Kay. I don't think it ever crossed my mind how I would manage all of that. I fully thought it possible for every single thing I wanted to come true. When I say I fully planned, I'm not really understating this. I had binders and lists and sections for each piece of my future. I'm pretty sure my Pottery Barn subscription started in high school. All my kids were named. I had even chosen my last name and practiced my signature in cursive. I thought a formal three-syllable last name would suit my lifestyle plans best.

Plot twist, real life happened. Of course, it is totally normal for the plans of a teen to not actually come to fruition. No blame there. Despite every carefully manicured scrapbook page, it didn't feel like I got to pick the details of my life. It picked me because suddenly I found myself in a place I didn't want at all. It didn't fit in my scrapbook or Pottery Barn catalog. It wasn't something I could even talk about at church, much less travel on stages for. My friends suddenly felt too good for me. I was trapped in a life I didn't want. A life too small for all the things I thought were mine.

'*Why did this happen? God must be mad at me. I'm not good enough.*' I always knew I wasn't good enough to be cool, and honestly I didn't even want that kind of cool. But 'youth group' cool, church level cool? Yea, I wanted that! I wanted the parents who were involved and all the kids went to their house. Their mom made waffles. The siblings did everything together. I wanted a group of lifelong friends. I wanted to grow up going to the same camp each year. It seems I wanted stability with a place to belong. Anyway, I knew I wasn't good enough for that and it felt like the truth just came out.

When I read Shauna Niequist's book, *Present Over Perfect*, I felt like I was reading about myself! This quote kills me:

"I don't want to get to the end of my life and look back and realize that the best thing about me was I was organized."

I want to actually try fun things and bravely experience the world, unafraid to fall.

So, fast forward ten years and my life looks pretty good. I married again to an incredible man who loves me well and loves God. We have two insanely awesome kids. This is starting to sound like The Wheel of Fortune, but let's continue. I graduated with my masters. I got an amazing job in our local hospital. My husband and I remodeled several houses. I plan lots of good outreaches at church and teach bible study and kids church. I sing in the band. I host a home group. I plan baby showers. I am room mom for the school. I love the Lord a lot. Worship music is always playing. I have good friends. My marriage is great, well pretty great. I mean, how do you even measure that? I love my life. I've worked really hard on it and it's all I could ask for really. Everyone tells me how amazing I am to be so busy. They constantly say they don't understand how I do all that I do and I respond with a smile and say I am just doing the things that are mine to do. I love it all and can't imagine not doing them.

> I know they say that about you too, because you are and you can do all the things, but you don't have to, to be amazing.

I go on to say that I'm really not that busy, I just do one thing at a time and enjoy every bit of it! I really want to defend myself here and all my mama friends who are in a similar place. (I hear you getting defensive. I get defensive every time I read this. I get it! You're just giving your kids a good life, doing what they love.) It's a good space. It really is happy. I was doing what I loved, I was taking my kids to do what they loved. We were creating memories and living full lives.

That's not true, at least three at a time.

Here's the thing. I didn't know what I was missing because of the busy. All the while I was running, I wasn't available to hear the Holy Spirit tell me who I am. I couldn't pay attention to my deeper longings or follow my curiosity. I tried to make space to invite others in because that is my love language. Not one of the official five, but give me inclusivity and some ten-inch baseboards and we can be fast friends. I invited them into my busy. Let's make sandwiches for the soup kitchen. Let's plan a party where I'll be so busy I don't actually talk to you. I realize I never planned that trip with friends. I never had that deep conversation with that person. It was all about accomplishing and completing my to-do list and I did it like a boss. The cost was high.

This whole journey started with the invitation to become still. I rebutted with tenacity! No thanks, just catch me on the go, God! I am really good at multitasking, I promise I can hear you while I work. My middle kid says this to me all the time and I can so hear myself in him. Patiently and steadily, for years (I am so stinkin' hard headed! I should have gotten this done years ago!), God kept inviting me to bring everything to him. Through those years I had to make space to hear. I had to make space to be still. I had to learn to be present. God didn't ask me to get honest about my questions, doubts, and fears because He wanted to embarrass me. He wanted to let me see that He would carry them for me, but I thought if I let that happen I would lose all of me.

I remember an afternoon when I was rocking on the front porch and my preteen joined me. We were able to talk about identity, where it comes from and how letting go of roles changes the way we feel. It can leave us uncertain about our purpose or how we navigate our days. The shift was happening family wide and my kids were given a chance to come up for air and really decide what it was they wanted or if they wanted something new. Life is about exploring your heart and seeing how that connects you to the Maker. We were learning that good things come to an end. We have choices to make every day for life and living. This one life goes so so quickly.

Through years of striving for the life of fairy tales, one line of thought remained constant beneath the ever-changing demands of life. Every event and lesson and revelation was filtered through a lens of teaching and sharing God's love with others. This vision and imagination remained unbothered by my seemingly errored ways. I journaled and dreamed as if I was still fifteen, young and full of courage. Then suddenly it was like I realized I was not fifteen. I was thirty-five and nothing in my life was as I imagined it to be. I was thinking the exact same way I thought as a dreaming teenager called to a higher life, but years passed and nothing tangible changed. Nothing that was happening on the outside aligned with how I thought of myself and everything suddenly felt wrong. Really really wrong. All of a sudden it was glaringly evident that I had missed a huge turn (we now know I am and was where I was meant to be) and wasn't at all where I wanted to be. There were red flags along the way. People who said how guarded I was, how hard it was to get to know me. In my mind, I would share my past on an as-needed basis. I wasn't hiding it on purpose, but it conveniently never came up.

This is for sure…

Truth is I was drowning in shame and was working my butt off to prove that I was still worth being used by God, still worth being noticed by church staff as important, still able to bring something of value to the world. I was too busy to know myself, too ashamed to be known, and hiding who I was because I felt unworthy. I lost myself in my past. I was still back there floating around, stuck in a time machine. I wanted to meet expectations but never could. I was so scared of being seen. In every church room I felt like people could see through me. They looked at me and knew I was dirty. That I had failed. Of course, I wasn't doing this on purpose! I was plowing forward in the wrong direction full of 100% energy and conviction. Wrongly. How can that be? I was fully convinced that I had put on my happy face and was doing a good job making the most of my situation. I was proud of myself in fact. *Wow, I really turned this around!*

My mom's best friend for many years was a second mother to me. We were at her house all of the time. I loved her three boys so deeply. They were military and so were we, so that gave us a common bond. When it was time for us to move in separate directions, she gave me a porcelain Precious Moments figurine. I can't get over the irony and find it especially intriguing because I cherished it so deeply as if it resonated directly with my heart. The doll was a clown putting on a mask and the label read PUT ON A HAPPY FACE. I connected to that miniature clown and put that mask on like it was my job. Putting on a happy face was my role in life. My nickname was Smiley Riley, so what other choice did I have?

2 Corinthians 4:2 (TPT)
We reject every shameful cover-up and refuse to resort to cunning trickery or distorting the Word of God. Instead, we open up our souls to you by presenting the truth to everyone's conscience in the sight and presence of God.

As I've gotten older, words have continued to shape who I am. I've certainly spent my life fitting into every crowd, shape shifting to whatever was needed. It's the art of the people pleaser. It goes so much farther than pleasing people. I think we should call it people impressing, people entertaining, or people worshiping. I can be charming and 100 percent engaged, but at what cost?

As I've gone through these years of unmasking, I've gotten so many comments:

"I like drinking Riley better."

"I like pregnant Riley better."

It's all in good fun, but when my whole identity is wrapped in how others perceive me, I don't know how to keep up with every request. If I'm better when I'm tired then I must be too much. If I'm better when I'm drinking, I am obviously not enough fun.

I've heard, "You look tired, are you mad at me? Sometimes you're sunny and sometimes you're quiet."

So somehow through the years of comments, I lost track of who I am supposed to be. Throw in some debatable topics of 2020 and there is no way for me to stand to please them all and so I shrink, sinking into worry and fear and anxiety. I loosen my grip on opinions. In my tendency to try to fix a situation and meet the expectation of who I am supposed to be, I make up my mind to be different. I won't be who they label me to be. I won't be "too" much of anything. I won't be bossy anymore during family game night. Really it's pride that results in shrinking me from being one who is seen and still loved. I can be loud or quiet and still loved. I can boss my way through a game and have so much fun and it doesn't have to steal anyone else's joy, because their joy is their responsibility. Being labeled doesn't box me in. I can value their comments and still enjoy myself and let my personality take up space.

In 2020, I was working my day job in a pediatric hospital clinic setting, so for a while we were furloughed. I mainly picked up weekends in the acute care hospital to keep us afloat financially but during the week, we were all home together. It took weeks for my body and mind to align in a space of less. For weeks my mind raced, whirling around trying to find something to do as we just took walks around our yard. Do we want to explore the driveway today or the back porch? It was such a weird time.

As a family, we had already been simplifying our schedule and cutting way back on responsibilities. We had been putting in the work to reduce our involvement and be more intentional about quiet space, but 2020 quiet space was next level isolation. I was so worried that by letting things go I would completely lose myself. I

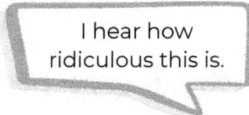
I hear how ridiculous this is.

literally had physical worry, like chest constricting pain and stomach butter-flies, that I would be boring and dull without all my roles.

Along with the COVID lockdown, I got to experience who I am without any roles. No church. No parties. No plans. Just me and the hubs and the two boys. Who am I here? Who is God to us without church? What do my kids know about life and God without outside influence?

It was incredible. I heard myself start to laugh. In this relaxed setting with all the quality time and without rush or distraction, we enjoyed each other immensely. I became more silly and creative. It blew my mind honestly. I didn't get lazier. Quite the opposite, I came alive.

God was showing me that from a place of rest and authenticity I can be the best me. The me my kids need. The me that loves well. The me I longed to be but didn't know how. At that time I had already been on the trip to rewrite the narrative of my life, so I was trying to navigate what my new life was supposed to look like. My mind was new but my actions were old. How do we take what is visible in our lives and align it with the intrinsic? How do we take off masks and live authentic lives? It's easy to agree, "I want to be real." I didn't want to strive or pretend or people please, but knowing *how* is a much harder concept.

Coming into the church scene slightly later in life, even though just in middle school, maybe I felt this need to catch up with those in the church. Early in my walk, I had set my vision on who I thought I was supposed to be and never took my eyes off of it in order to actually look around. I set my goal on being a good Christian and that idea took off, but it was that very effort that sidetracked me from letting God meet me moment by moment directing my heart and my steps. Though my motivation seemed pure, the act of being Godly became my problem. I wanted the real thing so badly.

This whole thing is such a mystery. The truth is I loved God with a desperation. I worshiped him and depended on Him with earnest striving. I clung as I should have and that slowly allowed truth to get in. It's the right thing to do. That was not fake. That was knowing where to cling. Surrender was a slow trickle. We can only surrender and confess as God reveals things to our hearts. He is gracious and patient.

I was slowly shifting my mindset, but changing my actions left me feeling lost. I had no idea where to put my energy. It's like the let down of emotions after the holiday rush. You go go go and have so much fun but then are just home in a routine and it feels flat. The house is drab without the evergreen tree and added snow globes and Santa figurines. I think I learned that a sad day doesn't make me a sad person. A boring day doesn't make me a boring person. Maybe I am not as entertained anymore by people's posts on socials doing every seasonal activity in matching family outfits. It lost its flavor. It took me a stupid long time to slow my mind, slow my expectations, and leave room for something new.

See, God is doing a new thing. Problem is it might look and feel like nothing, or even feel like your whole self is dying. How can waking up feel so much like sleeping? But I don't base my future or my belief on what I can see. I don't fill my worth up with what I can do or see. Research shows that kids need boredom to build cognition and creativity. This means they discover their worth and life in the quiet! Adults must need the same space. I needed that space to know myself, hear my thoughts, create my own thoughts even! I especially needed the space to let God nourish me and guide me.

> I don't base my future or my belief on what I can see. I don't fill my worth up with what I can or do see.

Away with the dark distractions
I wanna hear what's true
The only words that matter
They come from You
I'll just be quiet
And let You speak through the silence
Here I am, no more hiding
You are in this moment, I won't fight it
I'll be quiet

Elevation Worship, Quiet

5

Delight Delivery Girl

I wish I had an etch-a-sketch to wash clean and rebuild. It's the paradoxical beauty of the college student. My oldest son is a senior in high school and can literally pick from the entire world what he wants to do. Problem is this sweet boy in almost a man body has only ideas with no set plan. The possibilities feel vast and it doesn't feel like beauty, only life-altering, madness-level stress!

If I had known at eighteen that every choice I made then would set my foundation for now, maybe I could have picked a little more carefully. On the contrary, I suppose that is the design, for us to not have it all figured out ahead of time and to only make one decision at a time. Is this why we are encouraged to abide and lean on the Lord? I'd say it's precisely the time for that! We have to live to know. Move to be moved. Step to find out. As Richard Rohr says, "We do not think ourselves into new ways of living. We live ourselves into new ways of thinking."

So it may feel like we are just bouncing round and round as we come alive to a deeper knowing and understanding that we can choose and that choice is good, giving even. Choose life. Choose to be awake. Choose to listen. Sometimes just plain choose to not listen at all and maybe risk being wrong. So is it wisdom to choose well or is wisdom making each choice with faith because only in living and moving can you find your next step? I've heard and I believe it to be true: clarity comes with action. The very real fact is no matter how careful you are, mistakes will be made and pivots will occur and that is indeed a good thing because it makes life interesting, full of people and experiences. Life is meant to be lived! Knowing, believing, and trusting it all belongs is such an open perspective to hold. It's a loosened grip on the outcome and an embracing of the wild ride. Remind me of this when I cringe at something I say in this text, because every time I read it I think of something different I wish I had said!

In each piece of it all there is so much purpose and meaning, because there is a holy center to life. There is mercy not only in the fall but also in the recovery, because of a holy grounding. This is immensely difficult to grasp as acceptable, but we come to God by doing it wrong and Richard Rohr, in *Everything Belongs*, says even the wrong belongs. It has to and we have to live and accept our reality. He describes this transformative pattern with such exquisite imagery of our life in a circle (pg. 27). I picture it as our life lived in something like rings or hoops. The edges or the outer circumference of this ring is our surface-level commitments, the busyness of our lives, our circumstances. As we live out these details fully experiencing pleasure, as well as suffering, it all points us to the center. Everything we do is inviting us toward the center, a place of the divine, knowing God. Here we find our truest self, our real human self, because that is realized in the Maker's presence. We spend endless energy on the outer surface-level things, but it is essential to learn how to move toward the center and this usually happens through prayer and/or suffering. Rohr says spirituality is the act of seeing.

In Luke 18, Jesus asked a blind man what he wanted Jesus to do. The man said clearly, "I want to see." We, too, can ask to be able to see. Is the stuff on the fringe of my life pointing me inward? How do I need to see my circumstances so that I am not swallowed whole by grief? How do I need to see so that I can parent with the full armor of God and the anointed power of the Holy Spirit? How do I need to see so that I can be the spouse and daughter and friend others need? Ultimately, how do I need to be able to see so that I know my soul is fixed in the center, cozy and unfazed, with the Creator of Heaven and Earth while everything else spins around me as it does, though so often unbidden?

I share all of this because I wrapped all my worth in things that shift and change and were dependent on my effort. This only produces comparison and exhaustion. How do we ever know when we did enough? There are so many symptoms in our lives that indicate lives consumed only on the edge. There is such freedom in accessing your true self, the self that you meet in the presence of your Maker, a self that does not crash around in the waves of life. It is not easily offended or hurt. It can see beyond what is visible.

Somewhere early in my journey God gave me a kind message, an invitation really, found in Revelations. It states, "You have a reputation for being good but you are dead." (Ouch!) It's like He is saying, "Wake up! Wake up! You are not done yet. Perfection is not finished; you're on a journey." If we aren't careful, we can think we have it all together. Rather, we very well are acquainted with the fact we do not have it together, yet we push on believing we must achieve in order to succeed. We can think the things we are doing are good, our measurements of success valid, but they are only distractions. This is not to devalue excellence in our lives. The difference is in the root of why we do things and how we can use excellence to build our identity or let it be a result of something pure. What is visible to us is a false reality. Wake up and see what is good and true and available to you, son and daughter of the King, the Creator of all life. He speaks and life is born. He restores and redeems broken things. I wish I had had the courage from the beginning to live boldly for the life I longed for. Instead of believing I could step into it with authority, because it was already mine, I thought I had to earn it.

I've always said I would 100% go back and live again and do it differently. I have this nagging expectation that everything should be as amazing as possible. I'm pretty sure my husband hates this about me. I want every family night to be epic. I want every gift for others to be something they swoon over. I want all things to be over the top. I want top effort and every moment used to the max.

Just kidding, it's got to be his favorite thing.

50

When I mess things up so badly that I can't fix them, it eats away at me. I like to tidy things up, to file them as done. I do not understand people who are just so thankful and wouldn't change their lives even though it had bad parts. I wanted a redo so badly! I wanted to go back and get it right and love my life. I wish I could have lived my life to the fullest! I want the experiences that come easier before you are hindered by family and bills, like travel and adventure. I really did want my life in an etch-a-sketch. I suppose at this point I have finally finally... no I think I'd still prefer to have done it a different way. But this is the way and this is where I am and there is no washing it away. I don't get to control this and make it look better. God is unveiling the beauty and paints this story into a canvas of so much depth that I couldn't create on my own. It all belongs. He paints my character as good.

Romans 4:8 (TPT)
What happy fulfillment is ahead for those whose rebellion has been forgiven and whose sins are covered by blood. What happy progress comes to them when they hear the Lord speak over them, "I will never hold your sins against you!"

Also true, there is a sort of rebuild. Etch-a-sketch is so 1990s. In any current video game, you never run out of lives or erase your play, you just respawn. Such a weird thing hearing your kids yell, "I spawned!" I remember playing Mario and having to collect all those coins for an extra life before I had to share the controller with my brother. Kids today have it so easy spawning all over the place!

I don't have to wash it all away in order to start choosing now for now. Choosing now for my future. Choosing life now for my kids. The beauty of Jesus. Gah, it's so beyond this saturated idea of beauty. It is absolutely wrecking. I want to be real about this. Jesus is absurd. Completely backwards. None of what he offers makes any sense. As sure as the sun rises, his love is new every morning. Every single day is new. A chance to stand up again. To choose again. Not to try again as if I know I'll fail. Wouldn't I just say screw it and do whatever came easy if that were the case? Choosing what gives me deep life and friendship and adventure and thrills the depths of my soul takes effort. It isn't the easiest path but it is the easiest choice because it's the most genuine way to live and it gives more energy than it takes.

Plus, He mostly just wants to use our weakness anyway.

It's like He looks at the scraps and says, "*Yea that's the part I want.*"

"Don't you want this fancy part?" I ask.

"*Nope. I like this stuff that looks like nothing.*"

I don't get it, but I have to admit I love it. If I could parent my children with this amount of grace, I would love to successfully infuse this truth that their weakest pieces are what make our home better because it gives us the opportunity to rely on one another, pray for one another, love deeper. When you fail, we can find how it can be used for good. When you have a need, you can tell us and we will walk in that need with you until it is met. What if we talked about brokenness and redemption on a regular basis?

We talk about effort in our house a lot. My husband and I don't exactly line up when it comes to how much effort or work something should require. If I didn't put in tons of effort, I won't think I did a good enough job. He is going to make whatever it is as excellent as possible with as little work as possible. He's a smartie and makes things look awfully easy. A simple example of my desire for that extra effort: I could take a Friday night and sit on the couch to watch TV, even as a whole family and it would be fine, quality time. We often choose something by National Geographic and will all be on the edges of our seats cheering for the puma to catch the llama. Putting in the extra effort to wrestle with the kids and laugh and go outside to throw a frisbee... those simple yeses take conscious effort but the rewards are huge. This play and connection unifies and builds trust.

I feel this way about birthday cakes. I could buy a simple cake and it would be fine or I can stay up all night and create something that will thrill my boy's heart. The cakes are what he talks about for years to come. Weird but true. That effort makes the party more fun. Not necessary but so worth it.

Delight, I think, is the word for this. I love delight, live for it really. Squeals and surprises, the "beyonds" of life. My mom and dad are experts at creating "beyond" moments. I want to produce these moments and hand them out to everyone. Can that be my job? A delight delivery girl!

Unfortunately, even right now my mind can't help but go to a dark place where, even with healing and seeking the Lord, there are things in life that don't feel like delight and we wonder if we can ever be fully in delight as long as that hindrance is there. It's a different book, but the answer is yes. Even then. The delight starts on the inside. Where only breath reaches. As you stretch and pull and hurt, you are grounded in what is true and good and real. All the details of life are making space to be able to see the beauty grow.

My husband has been practicing delight in these years of coming together to create our life. Many years ago I would frequently drive by a local cotton mill that had absolutely burnt to the ground. I'd drive by just for a visit. The yard was covered in

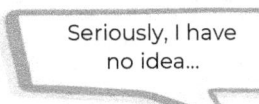

Seriously, I have no idea...

timbers and bricks overgrown in weeds but three columns built from bricks remained. Remnants of beauty standing tall against destruction. These columns were probably ten feet tall, maybe fifteen. They were probably only three to four bricks wide each and the bricks were covered in chipped turquoise paint. The top edges were broken off like you had bit your popsicle stick. I don't know how or why they stood like that—resolute, gorgeous, a reflection of what was. A place of depth and character. That's what I was thinking about as I passed the alluring towers on my left when I suddenly hit the curb on the right and heard a loud pop or two. I had to call my husband to rescue me. I told him how he was my hero as he changed my back tire, while rain drenched his work clothes and ran down his face, so that when I sweetly encouraged him to check the front tire too, he wouldn't be as mad. You gotta confess these things in small increments. I never fail small!

I wanted those columns. In fact, I *needed* them, badly. I begged Josh to go get them somehow. It just wasn't possible. Most things he can make possible but that wasn't one of them, until it was. He made it possible in the most surprising way. For my birthday he gave me a giant wrapped gift. Could those columns fit in that box, I wondered? Actually by that time I had forgotten about my demand for enormous mill-size columns to come home with me, so when I opened the box and had three column-shaped canvases with photographs of my beloved columns I absolutely couldn't believe it!! He even brought home a few bricks. More than that he gathered wood from the yard and built us a custom twelve-foot dining room table. Above and beyond, my man makes dreams come true and he is my true delight. How much more does the Lord give good gifts?

Proverbs 8:34 (TPT)
If you wait at wisdom's doorway, longing to hear a word for every day, joy will break forth within you as you listen for what I'll say, For the fountain of life pours into you every time that you find me, and this is the secret of growing in the delight and the favor of the Lord.

Delight or thrill is in God's voice, His word that speaks to me each day. It pours life into my soul, makes me come alive! The study of God's word shows me who He is, His heart for humanity. I can watch memes and Tiktok and read carousels on Instagram all about God or debating if the Bible means this when it says that, but all of that causes me more anxiety and even feels like info overload. When I am directly reading the Bible and find something new and realize for the umpteenth time that God is pursuing individual persons to show them their value, I get fired up about life! This is what makes life worth all the effort. Every effort, whether it's a humble apology or a fancy birthday cake, is pursuing the heart of the ones we cherish. Effort is laying down self, laying down comfort, for the one who needs love. Effort brings delight and says "you're worth it."

The earth is such a display of the magnificence of who our Creator is, his effort for us. His passion for humans and life is written and painted and demonstrated in every bug and plant. His wonder is for all to see from the rotation of planets to the creation of a baby. He has given all of that for us to learn to see, learn to live in awe. Proverbs 9:10 says: "the starting point for acquiring wisdom is to be consumed with awe as you worship Jehovah God." Over and over, life makes room for us to find him. When we feel there is no space for who we are, look again to the One who takes delight in every detail of creation. In every carefully created detail of you. The Father clearly delights in humans.

This new belief system became a place of rest for me. All of my life flows from this belief. I believe that He is happy with me. This belief alone gives me the freedom and space to be exactly who I am meant to be, who I want to be. Believing that who I am at my core is designed by God and that His intention for me is good. He gives gifts that are beyond good, they are perfect just for me, and for me that is seeing beyond what is visible. It is a deep knowing. He knows me and wants what is good for me, even as I go through life making all kinds of choices, He is also there, filling my life with paths to seeing.

525,600 minutes, 525,000 moments so dear.

525,600 minutes — how do you measure, measure a year?

In daylights, in sunsets, in midnights, in cups of coffee,

In inches, in miles, in laughter, in strife.

In 525,600 minutes — how do you measure a year in the life?

How about love? How about love?

How above love? Measure in love.

Seasons of love.

Rent, Seasons of Love

6

Meeting Joshua

Going to the performing arts theater was an extravagant treat. One of our favorites was scheduled to be there and a friend was in the show. We were absolutely elated to see it, but when we got there we were shocked to learn this local production was sold out. The stoic ticket person said we could wait around and grab tickets last minute as they become available. Josh knew how excited I was to see the show so really out of character he didn't give me much detail, kept it a bit mysterious but with confidence he was just handling it. No discussion or worrying. Just taking a 'my wife wants this and I'm making it happen' mentality. It's probably a top favorite memory with him.

My favorite mentality, by the way.

He went back to the booth while I waited hopeful and anxious on the bench. He came back after two visits. This time he was a little white in the face but also pleased with himself and standing a little taller. He took my hand and proudly walked me into the theater. Basically he was saying, 'Just enjoy, don't ask any questions.' Past the balcony entrance, where we usually get our cheap seats, and with gratitude. Past the founders' circle and all the way hand-in-hand quiet, anxious with awe and disbelief at this enormous opportunity, the very last seats available, the tickets my man snatched up and fought for just for me, were third row, front and center on the floor.

I've never had seats like that before or since. Seats so good that in the opening scene we could easily see the shiny glare of the patent leather shoes in the opening act of the show. I'm pretty sure both sets of our wide eyes could be seen reflecting from those glossy shoes. Our eyes widened even more as they slowly traveled up the performer's long black slacks, before fully noticing the costume of black tuxedos, then how the stage filled with a line of men who started to sing in dazzling harmonies. It must have been two songs into the musical that it finally started to sink in that this was not staged as a New York alley and there would likely be no off-color use of slang or social issues addressed in this show at all. As the jazz hands and blending of pop melodies pierced our ears, we, with equal shock, started to take in the advanced ages of those around us. I think what shook us from our confused trance were the much older ladies jumping up in front of us shaking their mature booties as they got tickled by the voices on stage, and maybe they were tickled by more than just the voices, but I couldn't tell you.

We held hands and slowly looked at each other, eventually daring to admit with a look that this was not the Broadway production, *Rent*, and that the tickets for *Frankie Valli & The Four Seasons* were astronomically more expensive than the small amount we had anticipated for the show that was being produced by a local company in the smaller theater next door. Do we stay or do we go? We paid for it. Also we're mid row, at least twenty seats to the left or right, so an exit would not be subtle. We finally conceded to the fact that this was miserable and could easily be the greatest fail of our very complicated start to marriage to date, and that's saying a lot. We slipped out, stepping on lots of polished toed shoes on our way. We hopped next door once we realized the error of our ways, presented our sob story to the doorman, and luckily were let right in for free, minus the hefty investment at the previous ticket booth to said stoic man. We were given free reign to any seat in the empty house so we chose to slip into the back row to watch the remainder of the local theater production. It was full of angst and we genuinely loved it! (Now that I think about it, we may need a redo on this plan, in NYC next time.)

I used to think this ambitious, high achieving man of mine was set on popping my balloons, just always telling me what to do and not do. I'm an idea girl and nothing pains me more than for someone to squish said ideas. And squish he would! He could come up with five reasons why my idea wouldn't work before I could finish telling why I loved it so much. And love it I do. Passion I do not lack! Every idea is my favorite idea ever and needs to be the best and biggest and done right away or I will just die. It took me a long time to see the depths of who he is and how all of that smart thinking he does gives me exactly the tether I need to actually be free. (Let me be clear here that this is quite ongoing: the learning to see and be and let be. Marriage seems to be a spinning circle of this process!)

I've given Joshua more grief than I care to admit in my relentless striving for happiness. We can call it perfection anywhere else in the book but at home it comes down to just plain wanting to be happy. We have enough striving for perfection in our house to fill a block. My striving is more of an effort to meet ideals and images. My idolized desire for a holy relationship, whatever that means, really just looks like me accusing him as if I'm his holy spirit. I let the belief slide in that if he improved himself, pursued God more, led better, or sought more counsel, it would fix our whole family. I spend a lot of time reminding myself that he is a normal man with his own past and future and that he is not intended nor expected to meet my every need. He needs my love as much as I need his. I spend even more time teaching our kids that we aren't perfect and if they want it they can look to Jesus. They'll never get it with these two control freak parents and we are just sorry. So sorry.

Despite my tendency to fall, Joshua is steady and that gives me safety and flight to my dreams. As we grow through the years I see all of his yeses. He might dissect my dream to the ground but it's so he can build it with excellence to help me succeed. Yes to house (as long as it's cheap), yes to trips (as long as he doesn't have to go), absolutely yes to this book (because what else is there), and yes to loving our babies with a greater intensity than we knew possible.

I confessed to him right away that I wasn't good enough for him, that I was a mess, but with easy confidence he said yes to me. We were miraculously on our first phone call after he had accidentally put my cell number in his phone wrong, one number off, and thrown the receipt, with my scribbled number, away. I was his family's server at Longhorn and please know handing out my number was absolutely not normal for me, but... well, I have no excuse. He was just so cute. I was sitting on the front porch of the house I had purchased for just me and it needed so much work. Sitting on the front porch was really the only appropriate spot for such an important chat. I'm not sure why he decided to go for it after my confession, because he definitely didn't know yet that I eat King Thin Sunbeam and Welch's grape jelly, just like he does. We definitely didn't know yet that we would never pee in front of each other or that we would really like the same church stuff: church music, preaching, all that, you know. Also, we didn't know yet that a double-sided mattress cover, one side that heats and one side stays cool, not only existed but would save our marriage, or at least the sleeping portion. So many things to learn after that initial commitment and luckily, he was just right for me. It's like God had something to do with it or something.

When we met, both of us were remodeling houses. This worked as a bit of a magnet bringing us into like-minded goals, because we were and are ultra goal oriented. He drove back and forth to Atlanta each week where he served kids with special needs. My squeal of glee that he did something with such compassion probably attributes to his hearing loss, though his superb skill at drums and bass likely lend itself moreso. He was coming home on the [and eating at Longhorn with his parents...] weekends to work on his house, purchased from his grandma Mema. The house was filled with memories and I'm a magnet to that. Then his long drives home became to work on my remodel project. He just simply stepped into that without hesitation, willing to come alongside and do anything to help. He got to know my dad on the metal roof. I'm pretty sure the story has something to do with him and my dad on the roof and one of them was covered in black paint!

Houses have always drawn me. This one was also full of memory, an iron bell at the door, and a mural painted on the dining room wall. It had one owner, who raised her children there; the garden was full of years of digging and sowing and reaping; and I wanted that long-term investment of growing children and flowers to rub off on me. I had never lived in a house for more than three years.

An understatement would be that this house, with its giant wrap-around porch, with wide wooden planked floors, painted green, was an ambitious project for me. On one of our first dates, we walked around the wrap-around porch to the back. I was showing him my back deck, which was really a wooden covering to park a car at the basement of the house. We leaned against the railing and stopped to chat about all the ambitiously planned projects when the railing completely gave way. As I was falling, full of panic, surely to my death, he instinctively reached out and snatched me, I kid you not. I'm pretty sure sparks flew in this heroic moment, strong and secure. Of course, we busted out laughing and immediately started planning a solution for the deck. And with that same confidence, he has said yes to me over and over again. He is equally exhausted by my ideas and elated to make me happy. I am forever grateful.

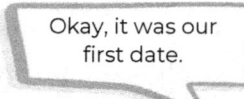
Okay, it was our first date.

Between my shadowed past and shadowed house, I thought this guy was a little crazy for jumping in. Just as he reached for me falling, his presence settled me then and it settles me now.

Unfortunately, and to my chagrin, my falling didn't stop there. I fell through the attic floor in our first house together. Grandma Mema's house. He was insistent that I not go in the attic alone. I was pregnant with our first baby and now I know he cared for me fiercely. Stubbornly I refused to be told what to do and promptly fell through the attic floor right through the brand new dining room ceiling. I ripped a hole into a life that was seemingly more perfect before I entered it. I would heed no advice. Headstrong, I couldn't see past my own nose. It took many more falls to learn to trust him and follow him.

You call me out upon the waters
The great unknown, where feet may fail
And there I find You in the mystery
In oceans deep my faith will stand
And I will call upon Your Name
And keep my eyes above the waves
When oceans rise
My soul will rest in Your embrace
For I am Yours and You are mine

Hillsong UNITED. Oceans

7
No Fear

I think I've spent my whole life trying to push out of wherever I am. Constantly in a state of resistance to what is. The whole time I was a kids' pastor I was fighting it. I didn't mean to sign up for that job. For as long as I can remember, I've been drawn to children. I loved babysitting and went to school to be a pediatric speech therapist, but it almost felt like I had outgrown the kid scene. I thought I was meant to be doing something different and that I was wasting time, stuck doing the kid thing.

Now I can see its purpose and beauty, a completely necessary step. The timing was impeccable and honestly very generous of the Lord. Teaching the kids was wildly fun and creative, with little pressure, but I knew He was calling me to something unnatural, where I would have to completely rely on Him. He used that easier thing to prepare me for this very hard thing. Instead of trusting the timing, I absolutely remained in a state of frenzy thinking I was behind. Always. That job felt like a distraction from what I was supposed to be doing. I stayed in a place of panic that I was missing out, missing it, late, too slow.

"You have no fear." Another one liner spoken to me that couldn't be further from the truth, but prophecy isn't making stuff up. It's speaking into existence what is. Worry, worry all the time, analyzing every detail. Can't I just settle in and trust I am where I am meant to be? Graham Cooke says prophecy creates momentum to propel you away from the foolish things of your life into the next chapter. It is how Heaven sees you and how you should practice seeing yourself. As you develop the language of

Heaven you see future and outcomes with anticipation. God is clearing your perspective so that you can see ahead.

This is how I became a kids' pastor without meaning to: As God was stirring up so much change in my life, challenging me to dig deeper, I felt a growing restlessness and a need for a new environment. We were deeply committed to and in love with the people in our church, where we had our hand in all the details of starting and growing this community. At one point we were involved or in charge of kids church, outreach, youth ministry, home groups, and music. A bit much, don't ya think? We wouldn't change a thing! We were passionate about it and were so grateful to be a part of it in that season.

Then when my dad planted a different church right in the middle of the poorest part of town with no band and no kids' ministry, I wanted to be there! At the initial meeting, there was so much energy in the room as he described his vision. "This is not an outreach, it is a lifestyle." I'm so in awe how he created a church from nothing. It was a dream and suddenly it was reality. A space for belonging. There was no band because each week he would invite a different person or group, with all varying styles of music, to come in and provide the worship. There were all types, let me tell you! This church was a full commitment kind of place, where there were no programs, simply obedient people listening and following God moment by moment to meet needs and build relationships. God used a few complicated situations to push us out of where we were and get us where we needed to be for that time. I can completely see now that, with this change in this fresh environment, I would identify my hidden hunger, my cravings, heal my heart, and renew my voice, my courage, to see my life, my story, my brokenness, as mission.

I had been wrestling with this idea of not being enough for my kids. I worried about what they knew about God outside of church. If there was no church who would God be to them? Is He just a thing in the sky that church talks about in simple worksheet stories that has no more impact except to tell them to be nice to their neighbor? If their dad and I were the only ones who ever talked to them about God what would they know? I wanted to be teaching them but just had no capacity for it and I wanted them to see God doing real things in real people.

I was so extremely tired of serving the church folk in circles. They (we) literally sit and absorb all the information week after week and we just serve each other round and round and round. We talk the same, eat the same, blah blah blah. I was exhausted and bored out of my mind. At the same time, I was searching for purpose in all my busyness and none of it satisfied. It was all good and nothing was good. I dared pen in my journal: "everything is good except spiritually." Well, yep. That's what happens when you run in a race with no end and no vision. It had to stop.

So off to downtown we went with no plan. No kids' church. No friends. No purpose except to find God in a new way. And that's what happened.

Stripped bare but clothed in a garment of praise. Our years at Artisan Church were exquisite. Messy and perhaps lonely. So extremely different, in the same town but nothing was the same. It was the simplest, purest beauty I've ever seen. My little one rolling cars on the floor with our friend, who happened to be homeless. My oldest chatting and laughing about the week with our friend, who happened to be homeless. Holidays spent with friends who lived in tents and lots of friends who didn't. We just were there together. There was no fancy kids' program. No youth group. No missions trips. We were on mission at all times. It was about creating family in the heart of need, knowing it, breathing it, and being together, because ultimately all of us share the same need for Jesus. Lives were dramatically changed, not because we were loving someone who lived in a tent but because we were equally loved by someone who lived in a tent. Radical love that flows both ways does that. I don't know how we got to be a part of something so powerful, but I wouldn't trade it for any programmed church experience. It was having a weekly meal as a church family that united and gave life. It was all kinds of people in and out, unpredictable at best, but always surprising with a story to tell!

When we got there I realized that my kids did in fact require some direct discipleship and since they were my kids I figured I needed to be the one to teach them! Weird to move across town just to spend Sundays teaching my own kids on a fold out table with a box of supplies brought from home. The space was concrete floors and the walls were lined with clothes on racks for donation night. That place turned into magic every Sunday. I didn't have a clue what I was doing. I didn't use a script or lessons. I just asked God what He wanted to tell the kids and then pulled it together in the most haphazard spontaneous ways. We had a blast! Every week we were doing something crazy, like setting things on fire, putting pantyhose over our heads, building the inner workings of the ear, or eating, I mean washing, pudding from each other's feet. Gross!

It was fun, because God is fun. It was scientific because God is a scientist. It was creative because He's an artist. It was curious and awe inspiring and it was always an invitation to the party. God's intention is to not dictate and limit our lives. I hate that we teach our kids these one line stories that shrink God into this far off thing in the sky that tells them what to do instead of mesmerizing them with creation and speaking into their existence that God is available to them in an intimate relationship! This time was really powerful for me not only as a parent, but it was practice for teaching and creating and growing my convictions. The world is ours to explore and cherish. We get to be in awe of so many things and people. There are a million differences yet each designed with precision and beauty. As a parent, teaching this passion about creation and life connected me to my kids with excitement. It united us in something outside of daily schedules. My confidence completely changed as I felt accomplished in providing them what they needed, also bringing balance to life's priorities. The amazing thing is, when I started planning these really fun things, I told God how cool it would be for more kids to come and guess what?! They did!

The kids at the church planned an urban garden party for other kids in one of the most poverty-stricken areas of town. We woke the sleepy street up every Monday for five summers. These people became family. My son begged for our family to move to that street, completely oblivious to the fears and prejudices others had in this space. The space was sacred and felt like a bubble where kids could be kids and dreams could be born. It was here that I really started to understand the brand new concept of going to where people are and not just creating things and inviting others into my schedule and my comfort.

Artisan Church was a place where racial lines and economic lines were blurred with one goal of loving one another. 'All are welcome' was lived out in the most practical daily display. My parents leading us all, working the hardest, and loving the deepest.

'Less is more' is so true. Despite its exquisite beauty, our season in this unique sanctuary was a pruning season. It was a time of removing some of our comforts in exchange for a genuine window into a different way God works. We showed up to this new environment equally apprehensive and excited but not ready at all. We had so much to learn and unlearn! My husband and I abandoned so many of our roles we had previously felt so attached to, leaving us floundering. We lost our social circles, leaving us stranded, but turning to one another.

We minimize trauma in order to be able to bear it, without breaking under its pressure. We reason through it, or maybe give it no thought at all, so that we can live with it, but there are hints that its imprint remains. Loneliness engulfed me again, triggered by a drive alone I took one Sunday to church. Writing the words can't encapsulate the level of panic with any logical understanding. Joshua had stayed home with a sick kid. Instead of appreciating his willingness to let me go to church and have the time for myself, I thought he was skipping out on church and rejecting me, as if those two things coincide automatically.

I've done many things alone, using huge courage. I've been the new kid walking into a class for the first time over and over and over. Only once did the principal find me in the halls crying and take me to the school kitchen for a fresh cookie right off the pan.

I've always been brave and independent, likely too much so. Isolated. That day, I feared I would have to muster a courage I had used many times before but everything in my body resisted. I had used it all up, years before, when I had attended church week after week alone, saving face, putting on my happy face, my everything-is-fine face. I know I am capable of doing really hard things, but with Joshua I just don't want to anymore. Somewhere between falling through the ceiling or off the porch railing and taking our recent leap into the unknown, I must have softened. I want to trust him, feel safe with him, know I'm his favorite, feel confident he will keep choosing me.

That day my wants didn't win. That day fear gripped me with a familiar squeeze that I wasn't worth being with. That this thing wasn't worth the effort it required. I wasn't worth that effort. I would be alone again. In some twisted way, when things feel too hard, I feel like that's a sign it must be right, as if I'm supposed to have to do really hard things. I'm supposed to have to fight. Is that how God wants things?

This move to the lonely wilderness, facing triggers, in fact, was the best thing that could have happened, because apparently finding my story would be like looking for your favorite shirt, thinking it's in the clean clothes, when actually it accidentally slid under the bed where it has collected all the dust bunnies, feeling impossible to find. I would need vast open space to work. God makes room in order to grow, prune, and strip. This pruning felt like it waxed my skin, leaving exposed every internal need for a soothing gel, but the relief would be slow to come. I had to become reacquainted with the hurt before I could receive that relief.

Funny how this waking I was doing felt a lot like dying, and how learning felt a lot like unlearning. Waking feels like a "Hush, child." disciplining, as things that felt precious and good were removed from my life. 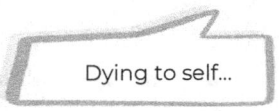 Trimming felt like doing less, doing nothing. It felt harsh and lonely and pointless at best. It was there, in that dreadful season of winter, I learned immense amounts about a million things I probably should have already known. I could only anticipate it would lead to fruitfulness, except at the time, I couldn't see the fruit. I couldn't measure any success because there was nothing being produced, as far as I could tell. I was only aware of my feelings and they were blinding, captivating my thoughts and tempting me to fall back into the normal hustle and grind. At least there I could get tired and could feel proud of my accom-43plishment. But, no.

The normal reached for me, begged me to come back to routine, to just be normal. Just be cool, talk about what's trendy, sign up, don't be the mom who gets left out. Feeling left out feels too familiar. My days are reduced to, "Just hanging at the house," because how do I explain to the outside that, "What am I doing?" looks like absolutely nothing, but my whole world is being rocked and the whole fancy production is happening in my head. The walls of my heart are shattering, but God is catching all the pieces and promises to make gold.

Beth Moore shares with such curiosity in her book, *Chasing Vines*, all about how the vinedresser sees so much more than quantity and quality when growing grapes. How she can write nineteen chapters about grapes and make us hang on to every fascinating word is genius. Grapes are apparently mentioned in the Bible thirty-three times! Whoa! God loves to watch things grow! This is evident and so the book is the richest invitation to know that "every last thing He plants in your life is intended for you to flourish in Him."

Within that deep promise is the harsh reality that the vine-dresser has the hard task to cut away what isn't producing and to make space for growth. Make space, there it is again. I think all God ever said to me for five years was, "*Make space! Clean out your house.*" So all my posts for months were about my five-minute drawer dump rule. I can drop that right here and now. If a drawer is bothering you, take five minutes to dump it as fast as you can. Put back what you need to keep and throw out the rest. Just like that, you've made progress in organizing. If it takes less than a minute to finish a task or walk the extra steps to put something away, then take the extra steps and go ahead and complete it. This will give such a feeling of satisfaction! A dopamine hit for sure! God didn't stop there, there's more! Clean out your life! Clean out your bills! Get open! Get ready for the catch! Is it okay for me to switch from puzzle pieces, to gold, to grapes and now balls?

My growth looked a lot like giving up, quitting, being quiet, and my worst nightmare: not being useful or feeling used by God. He eventually clued me in that He just wanted me without my usefulness. Okay, fine. "The only way you know God wasn't killing you is that a good many years later, you're still not dead." Thanks, Beth! (pg. 147).

Are things rarely as they seem in people's lives? We make so many assumptions about what others should or shouldn't be doing, but shouldn't we be giving the benefit at all times? How could we possibly judge someone or know all they endure or think or face? We simplify their lives to a place within our own understanding and we hold their life and choices against our hardest thing and our own level of overcoming. I wish I could remember to lavishly love each person, assuming they need it, because pruning in any season is not fun. Suffering is not exclusive to "those people" who deserve it. And we all long to find the treasures. The one not seeming like they are in need is likely the one needing it the most.

Beth Moore goes on to say (and maybe this will be my last Beth quote), "Anything He cuts off is to give breathing space to what He's adding on" (pg. 149).

As I let go of things that were so important to me just months earlier, I felt I was being completely stripped of all value and worth. I didn't know how to talk anymore without a list of tasks to talk about. I didn't know how to sound important or to show my contribution when I wasn't contributing. Slowly slowly slowly God was helping me find a safe place to bring my honest self, all my questions and

> Slowly slowly slowly God was helping me find a safe place to bring my honest self.

doubts, all my what ifs, my need for control, my need to use time, my fear of missing out, my need to know the details. I had never paid attention to these things in my life.

It is really crazy to look back at this time as a pruning season, but it for sure was. At the same time as I look back and think of all the details, there are abundant rivers of life. One year the Artisan kids completed jobs each week for the church in order to earn real dollars then spent them to furnish one of our church family member's new home, which was right next to the garden. They were ecstatic to give Ms. Charlotte all the best stuff they had picked for her! They also stocked her drawer with her favorite gum! I wish I could go back and savor these moments again.

It is fascinating to me time and again that as I explore my story, I find layers upon layers of love pursuing. It is as if the layers are living and active, God inspired. In the church, we have become comfortable with this language of pruning. It sounds rather old, doesn't it? Like prune juice. I'd rather be blooming, but no one asked me how long I'd prefer to bloom before I prune. Anyway, we could also describe pruning as a time in life when things don't go as expected. Losses occur. Things change. It can feel out of control and lacking in direction. It is a time that elicits showing up to the things you know to do and may be holding on to for dear life.

said with a squishy face...

Yet, as I look back at my "pruning" season, I realize it was happening in a real garden, where things are pruned so that new things can grow. It's so beautiful.

As we literally pulled weeds and buried seeds, we made space for children. This turning of soil offered them a new mold for living. I wasn't often the one pulling weeds, I should confess. I usually was holding arm loads of game supplies and sidewalk chalk. Nonetheless, it was a space of gardening, and we were seeing things be removed and seeing things grow in soil as much as in lives. My life, in fact.

It was a time to dig out the weeds that threatened my future. This pruning also created a new mold for my life at home and for my children's lives. Ordinary things like Sunday lunches, with this church family, were just breathing space for establishing holy habits. This is worship, where life is happening. Cleaning the dishes, wiping the spills, filling the plates, it all belongs in shaping us toward love.

I often come back to asking for the purpose of all this growing and seeking and stretching. Why not just love what I've got and live out my days? Unfortunately, our lives are not stagnant pieces allowed to float by unscathed. Rather there is a fight for our voices and our futures and we must actively seek truth and make space for worship. Our worship, which may only look like breathing room, and feel like nothing but making space for more spills, is extremely powerful in our battle against everything set out to steal what is good and true. The truth we long for may seem hidden, but it can be found in the garden. How well we prune is how well we grow.

Into the unknown
Into the unknown
Into the unknown
What do you want?
Cause you've been keeping me awake
Are you here to distract me
So I make a big mistake?
Or are you someone out there
Who's a little bit like me?
Who knows deep down
I'm not where I'm meant to be?

Frozen II

8
My Best Yes

Every major life change seems to happen when I am in my bed, and there I was again. God finds me best there, obviously, waking me to share some fun ideas. I think it must be the only time I'm still and the world around me is hushed. Has anything from God ever not happened in my bed? Like two things. This time it was more of a tortuous calling. Maybe not Moses-level drama, but enough for me to know He meant business. "It's time to give it up. It's time to tell the truth. It's time to be willing to tell your story."

Now important to note, I had no actual place to do this. There was no opportunity. I had no clue what I was saying yes to, but right there in that moment—one of many many many other moments—I finally said yes. So, so subtle but there was an insane beating heart in my chest. I knew it was different. I knew I had never said that to God before. It didn't matter how many times I had sung a song of surrender to God or told Him I'd do anything for Him. I knew those moments before meant anything *but* my story, and I knew in that waking moment, my heart was changed forever.

Funny thing about story is you have to know it to tell it. What I didn't know was that I had so much to learn. Knowing the punch line of a joke is one thing but coming to know yourself is basically an act of war. Seeing and seeking truth brings a full battle. So ensued a journey of seeking. That tiny whispered yes didn't change a single visible thing on the outside. It didn't throw me into a book or onto a stage (thank God!). It led me to a million more tiny yeses and the slowest journey of creation I've ever heard. This was not seven steps in seven days with some rest. Slow is an understatement but apparently my numb heart took lots of cracking. In *Present Over Perfect*, Shauna Niequist says, "Present is living with your feet firmly grounded in reality, pale and uncertain as it may seem. Present is choosing to believe that your own life is worth investing deeply in, instead of waiting for some rare miracle or fairytale. Present means we understand that the here and now is sacred, sacramental, threaded through with divinity even in its plainness. Especially in its plainness."

The first time I was ever invited to speak was for a women's brunch. That sounds fancy doesn't it? I know, and I wish it was. Invite me and I'll come to yours and it will be fancier than this one. This one was at my own church and I was invited by my own mom and the room was full of my very own friends... nothing special, right?

Except it was exceptionally special because it unlocked my heart. Well, actually it unlocked my voice. I spent weeks writing my story. It was my first time ever speaking it out loud in front of more than one or two people. The real big deal was that my mom would be there. Even though she lived my whole story with me, I didn't want her to know that I had actually, you know, "done it" or, in fact, made any mistakes. In my family—we tended to live in a bit of bliss. You know, like that line from *Wicked*, "You're perfect, no you're perfect, so we're perfect together. Born to be forever. Dancing through life!" Spoiler: the perfect one is fake and loses her friends and doesn't get that dream guy. The end.

So even though my mom knew I wasn't perfect, we never actually talked about me not being perfect and I thought maybe she still thought I was. That maybe I had miraculously met her and my dad's hopes for a perfect kid. We also never, not once, talked about the magical fun on Christmas morning being wonderfully magical *and pretend* fun.

Don't make me say it here. She's going to read this!

Seriously, not once in my life did we ever confess that we knew the secret. We just played along and had a blissfully merry time. It was wonderful. I genuinely loved and savored it and didn't realize that maybe it could be done a little differently until about yesterday. I especially recall when it was time for me and Joshua to get home on Christmas Eve to create magic for our little guy and it was so weird telling my parents. I'm only slightly dramatizing this! That truly was one of my favorite nights as a parent. Oh I love the Christmas magic!

Listen! I'm not blaming them one bit. I just had my third kid and I was still holding out for the one who would be perfect. It was so sobering the day she started demanding her own way and I realized we had another sinner on our hands. I try really really really hard to give my teenager space to be human, but for some reason it's ridiculously hard and I just want to save him from all pain and I want him to be perfect. Not for my sake, but for his! I want him to love all that life offers and have so much fun, but being human *is* participating in all that life offers. I'm always aghast but deeply curious about TV shows that showcase this concept of living so well. "When in Paris"—experience, live, make mistakes, ah the romantic life—if only, in reality, it didn't leave a trail of heartache.

I leave no room for that in my life, except it seems to find me despite my best efforts to be, well, perfect. Gah, what is perfect anyway? Could it be that I missed what a perfect life is supposed to look like? Is perfect holy? Or is it a life well lived? Have you even lived if you don't mess up? Hmmm...

> Did I dare just say that to my teenager? Yes, yes I did.

Shauna goes on to also ask, "What kills a soul? Exhaustion, secret keeping, image management. And what brings a soul back from the dead? Honesty, connection, grace". Perfection, or even the goal of perfection, brought nothing but loneliness and a longing to let it all go. I started to find freedom when I started recognizing the patterns and accepting grace. All of this happened as a result of seeking the Lord in my own story!

So I prepared for that church brunch for weeks. I wanted every word to be just right. I wanted to save face by making myself look gifted and called to speak despite the reality that the words I was sharing were throwing me under the bus!

Definitely still aiming for perfection here. I'm a hard nut to crack, in total denial that I won't make it! I'll die trying.

In prep for my message, titled, "His Voice", dramatically spoken in the voice of Ursula, I was walking through the dark house obnoxiously singing the aforementioned song. My oldest son was a preteen at the time, in 2018, and questioned what on earth I was doing. Stress relief, worrying, it must have been some form of comic relief. He was standing at the top of the stairs looking down and I was at the bottom late at night with his dad out of town; we had the most beautiful and unexpected conversation. I shared pieces of my story and ways that God had covered me again and again. Grey summed up worst-case scenario for me, "The room will laugh, and the world will explode," referencing his favorite cartoon, *Phineas and Ferb*. We had fits of laughter and were both very much crying (Grey always cries if someone else is crying), but the part I can't get over is when he said, "I'm your covering right now." And in that moment he absolutely was. God gave us that moment as such a beautiful image of what is possible with connection. It heals both people because of receiving help but also because of having purpose and being needed. Honesty makes space for that. My son is my brother in Christ and aside from all other details of life, that detail sustains me and gives me the greatest delight.

So much has happened since that December morning where chains were loosed and I learned firsthand that freedom comes, not just in hearing the truth that Jesus took my place on the cross so that I can live forever in peace with Him, but equally so in the telling of truth, speaking the word of God. The word of God is the written word found in the Bible, but also His living word spoken to me. Taking His fresh word for today that is spoken just to me and into my situation, allowing it to blanket my humanity filling my immense need for Him, brings a peace beyond explanation. Sharing this experience gives God glory and sets my heart free in a way nothing else can.

I don't want to wait until the end of this story for you to read that we are invited to dance with Jesus as co-heir and creator in this life. Connection to God ignites in the surrender of our humanity in exchange for the purity Jesus offers. Life explodes in billions of sparkles and invitations when we lay down our fear of rejection and fear of shame and pick up God's way. The thrill begins. The possibilities are endless. I'm not giving permission to live that romantic carefree life we see on TV that brings deep echoes of the heart longing for love, but instead it's the thrills that can only be found in  finding identity and life beyond pleasing others. The thrills in awakening the deepest desires of your heart, digging into the depths of who you are made to be and following that with curiosity and exploration and wonder. Thrill comes in trying out your voice and hearing the beauty of your Creator in it: full of purpose and life that can't help but contagiously invite others in. That's the romantic dance God welcomes us into.

This image of Eden contains a flowing and circular connection. Eden represents God's presence, full of Truth, His voice. Nothing hidden. Nothing made small. Nothing left wanting. Creative and alive. We all say, "Sure, sign me up!" It is in this blissful encounter with Jesus we feel so alive, clear minded, and ready for action. Eden gives identity and confidence that removes all comparison. Achieving will always lend itself to further comparison. Only when we abide in the Father and flow from a place of intrinsic contentment and purpose will any of our "works" be satisfying. Heaven on earth is in each heart. He prepared a place for you and it is now. Heaven is here, Jesus is here, in your heart, in your life. Active and moving and breathing life, guiding and giving generously. Instead of looking for Him in a revival moment, find Him in the real-life moments. This is where you will find your transformation.

Not to say we aren't still on Earth, obviously. The kingdom of Heaven is real and so we pray and set our minds in the spiritual realm, but there is also very much Earth and all of its complicated hardships that seem to press us on all sides.

There is grace for that. There is peace in the chaos. There is softening in the hard. There is a balancing of what we can see with the love we know at our core. It's learning to walk in the dark. To be in this life but not of it. How do we carry the tension of humanity while keeping the spiritual realm as our reality? It feels like there is no separation. We are constantly bombarded by this full immersion into humanity that feels overpowering. We feel the darkness. We live in our own dust, yet full of life, full of hope and full of truth. It's another paradox of being full of what's true and fully clothed in Truth. We might be immersed in a culture of rampant evil but within us is the breath of life and surely nothing can be more powerful than that.

It's mind-blowing and bizarre for me to think about how long before my "rewrite your story" trip, well before my best yes—the surrender—I had been moving toward the moment of actually sharing my story. I mean, it was forever. It was like my whole life led to it, honestly. More specifically, God really started getting my attention toward *something new* around 2013.

During that time, I had our second baby, my husband had major back surgery, and my aunt passed away from cancer, which sent me into a spiritual crisis I had never faced before. I questioned everything and felt at such a loss for answers. My foundation was swiped and I realized how little I knew about what I really believed. I really felt drawn to host a bible study/book club and even though I wanted to do it, I faced immense fear of rejection. I'm not talking about nerves from thinking of providing refreshments or worrying that no one would show up or the women would talk too little. I am talking full blown physical panic that these people would see me for who I really am. They would see my sins exposed and know how horrible of a person I am. They would know my doubt and my stupidity and that I never measure up to a single thing I'm teaching.

I journaled about it for weeks, tortured that I couldn't handle the role. I remember to this day confessing to the group that I was divorced. I vividly recall the moment taking at least five minutes, because I was mute with a giant rock in my throat, absolutely paralyzed by fear. Surprisingly, no one got up and left or quit the group. I had no voice and no foundation of grace. My perfection wouldn't allow grace to stick. Donald Miller in his memoir, *So Close* said, "Grace only sticks to our imperfections. Those who can't accept their imperfections can't accept grace either."

I was completely swamped in confusion with questions like, "Does God actually want me to fail? Is He trying to embarrass me?" I felt as if I were on the edge of a cliff and I was supposed to jump. The problem was that my faith had little substance. In the parlor of my home, full of beautiful friendly faces, then again at the brunch, my mindset was still very self-protecting. Those acts of faith were mustered up by sheer will power, especially at the book club. Looking back, I'm not sure it was the right time for me to share that. I wasn't safe at all in the Lord. I was only fearful of the people. At the brunch, God had certainly started giving me courage, but I was soon to find out the journey healing would require.

> That's what we called it for fun.

The wind is howling like this swirling storm inside
Couldn't keep it in, heaven knows I tried
Don't let them in, don't let them see
Be the good girl you always have to be
Conceal, don't feel, don't let them know
Well, now they know
Let it go, let it go

Frozen

Walk in the Dark

Just to set a clear timeline, it all started with the book club bust. It would be several more years before I actually laid down my fear and trusted the Lord with my story by sharing it at the church brunch. I actually went on to start a podcast for story sharing (how things change!), but before I did that and after the women's brunch, I took a trip.

I whispered that meek, "Yes," surrendering my story, and was terrified I would be thrust into the light. Not so different from a dream someone has about singing on Broadway, where the spotlight is awkwardly bright. I really must have thought awful things about God, like He was out to torture me. Nope, I wasn't put on a stage, thank His kind heart. Instead, I was sent on this bizarre trip. The trip was the first way I learned about what it means to seek God in my own story, but, of course, I didn't know any of that going in.

I had just shared at the women's brunch at my church and was on a high, feeling some relief from the burden of secrets and the heaviness that comes with them. I didn't know what came next. Was this my one big act for fulfilling that nagging purpose and now I could get back to menu planning and soccer games? I was asking God about it and felt this strong need to go visit a few people from my past to practice telling my story, to apologize, set things right, and get their perspectives.

At that point, I was not free from shame. In fact, I was physically feeling the effects of shame and just could not tell my story without sobbing. I loathed everything about it. Ultimately, I loathed myself. I hated my story. I hated that I had ruined my life. I hated that I had hurt other people. I was parenting from a place of fear and approached marriage and friendships the same way. I would have done anything for a redo. I knew nothing of what it meant to make mistakes and use them, and allow them to grow you. Celebrate them even. I feel super embarrassed that I reacted that way. It felt too big a reaction, too much a response to failure. It felt like I should have just been able to brush them off as young love and move on. People do lots and lots of things like what I did and "worse" so looking back, I tend to think, '*What in the world was the big deal?*'

If I tell you about my "sins", most people wouldn't think much about it. Some would think I hadn't done anything wrong at all! They'd tell me about five other people they know who went through something similar, and I have no idea how those people feel, but likely if they believe in God and make any attempt to align with Him, they are going to feel remorse and shame over the failed union or whatever other selfish impulsive decision was made.

Sin is the trickiest piece of life. It feels like nighttime. In the night sometimes I have this dream, recurring, where pieces of me feel giant. Sometimes it's my lips or my hands that feel swollen, like a bad reaction, and everything around me feels teeny. It reminds me how at night my mind races and I can't always find a solution, then when morning comes and routine begins again, whatever was bothering me isn't so looming.

Shame feels like night. All is so dark making it hard to see a next step so I start rationalizing how to put things back in order, as I expect them to be. I struggle so much to be comfortable letting the mess coexist with my joy because ultimately I believe my peace and joy and dreamy happiness is to be achieved and no matter how much I hear it, my body won't let me settle in a space of contentment when something is not as it should be.

God makes space for it. From the beginning He made space for it, knew it was coming, in fact, He expects it. It's me who acts so surprised when something isn't right. I try and try and try to fix it. To make it presentable, manageable, at least decent! Kind of like when I pinch my cheeks for a little color. Just let me look alive!

The problem with the unexpected is we feel completely alone. Isolated. Broken. This magnifies our problem until we feel all will stare and judge and assume and conclude. We twist this thing to be bigger than it is. As I write this book I can't decide if I'm okay with sharing the weight my mistakes created or downplay them to prevent looking too sensitive. I don't want to talk about myself too much as if my life is worth entertaining you. Yet the greater point is we all have things that loom like giants and fear they may take over our very existence. They take bigger space than they deserve, directing our logic and clear thinking. We aren't alone in these fears. I don't actually know what to do except to bring

> Tell. Connect. Courageously be known.

it to the light. Wake up. Let morning shine on it. Tell, connect, courageously be known.

I feel completely silly writing these things down and being known by them, so much so that I repeat multiple times that I'm probably the only one who worries about this or gets upset about that. What's important I mean, maybe I am the only one who worries about compulsively driving off a bridge. I mean, I'm not saying I want to, but what if I just do by accident? Surely, I am not the only one who feels like a horrible mom when my kids are eating fast food and the mom next to me packed a wholesome picnic. Then the secret of all secrets, am I the only one who tries to hide when a sneeze-poot sneaks out? What's important to

> Hello third kid problems, or maybe it's being 40?

note is that each of us feels isolated for something and the point isn't to compare levels of trauma. We walk a journey far from home and long to have love meet us in an embrace saying I see all of you and I made space for it. Come let love wash you, hold you, bring everything into perspective.

When I compare my life to others, I can feel especially stupid for hurting. I don't pretend to have it all figured out. I haven't thoroughly explored all the nuances of these happenings, but I do know with confidence that I was hurting and lost and that God showed me a new way. He covers me with fresh water.

When God directed me to go back in time on those trips, all other creative flow stopped. It was like my mind went blank. I had no words. No creativity. No nothing. Honestly it was pretty cool to realize that I was given that direction and all else was on hold until I started the journey. There was no distraction, no noise, no debate. Go. End of discussion.

Isn't it so true: God speaks, and we are like, "Okay, team God! On it! Yes, let's go!" A day or two passes and we're like, "Oh no, God, where are you? Why aren't you talking to me? I feel so lost and alone, suddenly frantic and desperate, without direction." Can't you just hear Him laughing kindly, thinking, '*I just gave that girl a task that will take at least three months, but instead of doing it she's in despair again*?!' Let's be a people who boldly carry out the mission set before us with a settled heart that God is for us, on our side, faithful to give every step we need. In addition, God is not just a task master barking out orders. Abiding in love can be simply abiding in the moment just for the sake of presence, soaking in peace, without any commands at all. All of this journey has brought me to a place of knowing He is near, right now. Breathe.

So I immediately planned a trip and of course the details were beautiful. My best friend from my Florida high school welcomed me into her home; her husband was already planning to be out of town. I remember waving goodbye to my boys as I pulled away down the driveway on my way to Florida. They were standing at the end of our southern front porch that spans the length of our house and wraps around the end of the house, where we pick figs from the top of the tree. They stood there, all together, with big sweet smiles that love me so well. They were waving big and yelling, "Bye!" None of us knew I'd come home a different person. I drove down late into the night. My husband is very protective. He told me not to wait too long to get gas and I scorned him, '*Of course I won't. I'm not stupid.*' Sure enough I was on that long country highway and had to turn around and go back twenty miles to be able to get gas because I waited too long and there were no more gas stations.

I am so scared of the dark. Truly. Even now fully grown. When my husband goes out of town I just stay up until I can't keep my eyes open any longer. While driving it got dark and then it started pouring. Not a little but a lot of rain. So much that I could only drive a few miles per hour: slow enough that someone could run to catch up with me and jump in my car! I was terrified! Unreasonably so. What if I had to stop or what if a monster gobbled me up?

In that drive, I turned on Beth Moore because she is like my spiritual mama and has literally walked with me via books and studies through every single season of my life. I turn to her for all comfort. I wish someone would tell her so we could just go ahead and start our in person friendship soon. K, thanks.

I don't know what was said exactly, but I think it was about fighting and how we can do hard things. What was for me loud and clear is that there is a girl on the other side of my healing who needs to see my scars. My healing is able to give life to someone else who is hurting. I've heard that there are no scars when you are healed and maybe that's true, but even Jesus showed Thomas his hands, and maybe I'm finally at a place where scars don't scare me. Instead let them bear witness that I am a conqueror.

Always a contrasting thought fighting for space in my head; simultaneously, I was fooled into believing that most people don't hurt or need help and are all so happy. That could be true, but I knew there are at least a few who do need love, a new narrative, and to undo some things. There must be a few who need someone to rescue them and show them a new way.

Suddenly walking through the dark felt worth it. After successfully driving through the dark, I felt ready to fight. This image became clearer to me over the next couple of years. I spent so much time avoiding the dark. I thought I needed to be happy and create joy and do my best when really what I needed was to get honest about the dark. I had to walk through the truth of what happened and let Jesus meet me in those places and bring peace to each hurt.

Walking in the dark is probably also debatable theology, but all I mean is that I had to get real. I couldn't pretend like all was well before letting myself grieve and feel and process. I didn't need to try harder. I needed to *trust* that God was my bright light and that He was a safe place to bring my honest and raw self, my broken and needy and ambitious and longing self. This is so so different from the idea of letting it go. Let it go? That's impossible. We all know that. It isn't about letting it go as unimportant or just in the past as if the past doesn't literally grow my future. It's about bringing it to the light so that God can hold us, so that He can take it and love us with it and use it.

When I spent time writing my story and reacquainting myself with the details, I discovered enormous treasures. I was in my lowest place alone and broken before I had moved home for the divorce. Again, I was in my bed, seeking the Lord and poring over Scripture when I knew it was

> When I spent time writing my story... I discovered enormous treasures.

time for me to leave. My brother had actually come to stay with me for the summer, so he was there, in my house, in such a time of need. When I told him I would be leaving, he held me tight and was there as love with skin to hold me in a very very dark time. Realizing, years later, that I actually wasn't alone and that God had provided a covering for me helped me see this story in a completely different light.

When I thought I lost me
You knew where I left me
You reintroduced me to Your love
You picked up all my pieces
Put me back together
You are the defender of my heart

Francesca Battistelli and Steffany Gretzinger, Defender

10
Time to Rebuild

Psalm 51:6, 12, and 16 (TPT)
I know that you delight to set your truth deep in my spirit. So come into the hidden places of my heart and teach me wisdom. Let my passion for life be restored, tasting joy in every breakthrough you bring to me.
For the source of your pleasure is not in my performance or the sacrifices I might offer to you. The fountain of your pleasure is found in the sacrifice of my shattered heart before you.

The next few months I spent rewriting the narrative of my life and learning to take off masks to become honest. Truest of true. It would undo me before restoration could come: completely etching my story and letting God breathe new life in.

This was before I really knew what God was up to. I just thought I was going to share my story with my friend who'd lived it with me, except she really wasn't there because while in survival mode I shut everyone out. I wanted to learn to talk about my pain with someone who I knew loved me a lot. A safe place before I shared it for the benefit of others, if God ever guided me to that again. Andrea was #1 on the list.

The first town on my 'Rewrite Your Story' list was the one that held the most memories. As I drove into the town, the effects of Hurricane Michael were everywhere. Trees were completely broken in half on both sides of the street, as if it was an intentional breaking, an attack. I can imagine the unexpected force of wind that wrecked the city that day and all the lives within.

The next morning, in the sunshine, I could see more evidence and it shocked me with a display that matched the torment of my heart, almost like those personality tests you take, when you feel like reading the results is exposing all your weaknesses. I'm not sure which I'm talking about when I say completely beaten down. Broken. And honestly, unable to be fixed. Are we referring to the city or my heart? I wasn't expecting this evidence to give away my secrets, to put my secrets on display.

I was so stricken by the devastation, I paused to write in my phone that day:

So much destruction. One storm.
It looks like my heart here.
Changed.
Learning to see, speak, hear truth in
the face of destruction.
So many memories.
The beach was dreamy.
The independence thrilling.
Romance, sand, friends.
There is no condemnation here.
Only Love.
My heart is open. Raw. Scared.
I didn't see that I was stepping into
destruction. It was all pretty things.
Be still and let me heal you.

The storm devastated everything. Almost every building had tarps on the roofs. The streets were lined with mounds of clothing, ruined furniture, and debris. Some buildings were completely blown out and were without walls, windows, or roofs. Church after church and business after business, closed. Isn't that how I had lived my life for the past ten+ years? Closed up, guarded, unavailable, but longing for more?

What I noticed as I explored the neighborhoods is that before we could rebuild, all the damage had to be pulled out. It may have looked really messy. There may have been a wet pile of mess and often there were many! What I also observed were crews and teams of people working in all kinds of places, even months later. It was beautiful to witness. I knew then that I had to choose to invest in my healing. I had to do the thing that felt selfish or time-consuming, which for me was ending the obligations that didn't serve my goal and taking the time to get to know myself once more. I know now that this investment would cost a lot and pull me away from the life I knew, but that it would give back a life that felt connected and aligned. I definitely relied on a tarp or two of prayer and friendship and leadership to cover me.

But you will rebuild. Signs of hope were as numerous as piles of trash, "Reopening Spring 2019". I was starting to see the work I needed to put into my own life. Pulling out the old to make space for new. I was starting to recognize the need to allow others to help me in ways I couldn't handle on my own. Putting on my happy face wasn't going to work anymore. I was undone.

So that day, as I shared with my insanely amazing friend for the first time in so long, I first got to the point in the story where I wanted to apologize for the ways I had caused her pain, including abandoning our friendship during my time of survival and desperation. It is devastating how trauma removes the capacity for friendship when that connection is the most life-giving thing you can have, but the Lord had given her understanding during that time and she chose loyalty to our relationship and to believe the best in me.

Without hesitation, with deep sincerity, Andrea unabashedly came over, hugged me, and said she had zero negative feelings against me. She sat so close, leaned in and spoke life back into my heart. She described our friendship as "connection". Together we are our best selves: fun, silly, young, carefree, and playful. It didn't matter how time passed, we were connected and what a powerful word that was. It must have been the word of greatest depth. Then after I said everything, confessed my longing to tell my story, she said, "Well of course! DUH! It is what you were made to do. I've been waiting for you to finally do it. This comes as no shock at all!"

I didn't realize the depth of regret, pain, and sorrow I felt over my friendship with this treasured friend. I told her I would go through it all again to spend more time with her, love her better, and have more fun. She is better than any fun imaginable, but she is actually the definition of fun and a giver of life. She showed what it looked like to do what is yours to do with excellence. Her friendship is such a gift. It felt really incredible to have her forgiveness.

A layer of my heart came back to life.

It's amazing what true connection produces. It's human nature to fear and run away from an unknown result. The tradeoff though is so lackluster and you end up missing out on so much goodness. I wonder how many relationships fizzle out because time causes it to fade or something small happens and no one puts forth effort to repair. Why do we let that happen? Relationships are worth fighting for. They hold the depths of life. I see Jesus in my friends. I know love because of their love for me. I understand resurrection and the healing life that is offered because of restored relationships. Hard things certainly have a way of exposing the trash and bringing forth beauty. This must be the meaning of victory. Hard fought-for victory.

So how did God rewrite my narrative with that interaction? He let me see that He sees me as fun! He is not surprised by my story and wants to use me to the fullest of my heart's desire! He is patient and understanding and full of love for me. Healing takes time but it is fully mine for the receiving. Now, how do I actually live the life I imagined?

Here's a little song I wrote
You might want to sing it note for note
Don't worry, be happy
In every life we have some trouble
But when you worry, you make it double
Don't worry, be happy
Don't worry, be happy now

Bobby McFerrin

11
Design Your Life

Is choice the whole thing? God set choice from the beginning and it is certainly one of the more complex components for us to understand. Free will with sovereignty is just bigger than I can grasp, but maybe it comes down to choosing to trust that whatever it is, God is good and He wants what is best for me. Is it a one-time choice to follow God? It has felt that way in church at times. Could I view it rather as a daily choice to live? To abide? To receive? To give? To love? To smile? To think? To pause? What would it produce to choose daily to believe in the best for me? What would it produce to choose to face the truth and build again? To choose to live again? Who could I be if I chose my actions in that way? It could be fun to take time to go back through life and write out choices.

Bear Grylls has an interactive show where the kids watching choose and the show is determined by their choice. If I had chosen this, then what? Or what will come if today I choose this? And not to a detrimental place of regret but more an observation and way to learn from the past... If I had gone to school there, what would I have wanted to learn? What club would I have joined? If I had pursued that friendship with boldness and said yes to that opportunity, where could I be now? If I choose this thing, whatever it might be, where will it land me in five years? Let the answers be a guide.

I remember being asked to shut my eyes and imagine my life in five years. Then to imagine if my life looks like it does right now, how will I feel? My blood pressure must have skyrocketed, because I immediately thought, '*Over my dead body will I be in this same place. I will not, I CANNOT be here doing these same mundane things.*'

Though it has been almost five years since then and life looks a lot the same—my floors still need mopping and laundry is a daily occurrence—I am not the same. Weird how a measurement of progress has so little to do with outward appearance.

I learned from a precious woman and friend who is a little farther along than me in life, Martha Hall, to pencil in whatever idea I have on the calendar. I soak in her gentle wisdom, always taking mental notes when she shares pieces of her life. Her advice was to go ahead and pick a day for that trip or to spend time with that friend. The time will eventually come, and you won't regret having it already on the calendar. If you wait for the right time, you'll never plan it and all you'll have is wishing and regret.

I took that to heart and had the most fun of my life that year. I spent intentional quality time doing the things I wanted with those I wanted. It was life changing. It was chosen. Thinking about what I wanted, what I valued and choosing it, I still forget to do that. I also decided to say, "Yes." If invited to something fun, say, "Yes." Don't worry about kids or schedule or whatever. Say, "Yes," believing there is a way. It has brought a lot more opportunity. I used to worry so much about the details: if I should leave my kids behind, or if I should or shouldn't spend the money. Short answer: I should, if I want to. There's nothing overly spiritual about that. It's choosing your life, while trusting God is in it and for you. Annie Dillard wrote, "The way we spend our days, is of course, how we spend our lives."

I learned through a combination of undoing things that weren't good for me and filling in God's word to spur me on toward the truth that, as a co-creator with God, I get to design my life. Yes, my life is His and I get to reflect Him in every choice, but also He has trusted me with it and says, "Create, choose, build a life." I get to pay attention to what gives me life and spend my time doing it. I am anchored by these things.

Doing doing doing things because they are expected and good and fun and everyone is doing them drains me and leaves me lifeless. Not only that, but that stuff blinds me to my purpose and distracts me from ever accomplishing anything I actually want. They are fun, wonderful things that are just completely wrong for me.

There is so much I want to expound upon on this topic, but I'll share a verse that impacts my view of this concept, well two:

Ephesians 2:10 (TPT)
We have become His poetry, a re-created people that will fulfill the destiny He has given each of us, for we are joined to Jesus, the Anointed One. Even before we were born, God planned in advance our destiny and the good works we would do to fulfill it.

Philippians 1:27 (TPT)
Whatever happens, keep living your lives based on the reality of the gospel of Christ, which reveals Him to others.

The way we live, the way we walk out the things of our hearts, the things that make us unique, makes God visible and brings Him close. This is the gospel of Jesus on display. The gospel, evident in us, brings joy and strengthens others. Don't ask me how! It's more than I deserve to know this much and I know so very little about it.

I ask a lot of questions about time. It's kind of weird. But for real, I want to know where time goes. Obsessed. Why don't I know what happened to it? How did fifteen years go by without me realizing it was passing? If my greatest fear is wasting time, then how can that happen to me? Do I want a life that is all a blur? What makes it blurry? Does raising kids have to be chaotic? Does it have to be a race for every Friday and a summer escape to the beach?

I don't want that. I want to use my time well and celebrate it. I want to thank time for giving me every year with my children. I don't want to come to an end, the end of 5th grade or the end of the balled-up baby stage or the end of high school and wonder what happened. I want to know. I want to know that I was intentional in staring at my children in the face and watching them sad or watching them happy. I have spent hours angry at my kids—rushing them to hurry up or finish or do this or else. It leaves me so depleted. I can't imagine how it leaves them. It's an odd mix of devotion to your kids and having your own outside purpose. It's really all the same.

Writing is my worship. I spent years believing that writing was very selfish and that it accomplished nothing. So when I wasn't working my day job, I would spend all my remaining time with my kids, doing whatever they were doing, which is very often throwing some sort of ball. I love to create moments of magic for them. I love to make every day count. The problem is I didn't pay attention when I felt a pull to be alone or spend time on myself. I always wanted to be available to them, undistracted, present. Regardless, I definitely will always choose jumping on the trampoline over cooking dinner. See how my priorities aren't exactly working out? Working out? That was off the table too—selfish. There was no balance in my priorities.

I finally discovered that without writing and studying, my emotions towards my kids would become resentful and I would be dull. When I live awake, using my passions, I give the best to my kids and show them an image of the Lord that can only be reflected by me. The Lord says to bring our best first in tithe. I agree this is financial, but I can't help but also think that my best is my story. It's all of me. Doing what is mine to do, in obedience and with excellence, is loving my kids first and best.

What does living awake even mean? Hunger for God above all else. This awakening must be recognizing the hunger of your heart. It is an intense craving, a longing for the richest pieces life has to offer. God wants to give these things out of His abundant passion for us. This is the land of the living that God desires for me and for you.

Psalms 27:13-14 (NIV)
I remain confident of this: I will see the goodness of the LORD in the land of the living. Wait for the LORD; be strong and take heart and wait for the LORD.

It means choosing what gives me life and taking action toward that. It means making space to be able to listen and see beyond the ordinary. It means letting go of what is stealing, absorbing, dampening, numbing. It is a place of being settled in knowing God is with you and for you. Closer than your breath, unwavering, and flowing from that connection. Flowing in gifts and passion, purpose. Listening today to hear His voice and walking in it, on mission, whatever that may be today. There is thrill in this life and I want to live like that. I want my kids to see that!

So there was a time of extreme, as things go. Just like my parents rid our house of all things ungodly, this was a season of ridding my life of all things that were not my one thing. Things got really quiet. No dinners, barely any friends. Just me journaling a million words and brain dumping over and over and over until it started to rebuild and piece together like the giant puzzles we completed during COVID.

It started so simple really. I thought when I said yes to God I would be thrust into the light but instead it looked like hiking. It looked like cleaning out my house. It was weekends playing in the yard. Searching for God is quiet work. Finding Him is even quieter.

God doesn't steal anything. He doesn't hinder or restrict to hurt us. He doesn't morph us by using manipulative language. In every detail He empowered me with strength and purity. He elicited integrity, being authentic. What a miraculous blend. He gave me a voice. He restored my worth. He beckoned words and language. Words of honesty, truth. This set me free. This was a season of making space to find my thoughts. To attach meaning to feelings and search the deepest parts of me to know me. So many questions asked of me were left unanswered as I learned my own voice. I didn't know many answers because I'd never taken time to answer them or give them notice. I constantly felt the fool but refused to quit pursuing. This season was soul wrenching as I wrestled to come up for air. My mouth felt mute but my heart burst with new life. Creating does that. It's a quiet work that bursts with energy. I kept choosing life, life, life again and again and slowly, slowly, ever so slowly put one word with another and learned how to talk about who I am, where I've been, and eventually where I am going. To dream again.

Finding God in the past showed me my future.

God wanted me to get honest. To make space and stop pretending!

Can I just say it plainly, because it feels tiring to add anything? God plain wanted me to get honest. To make space and stop pretending!

2 Corinthians 4:2 is an amazing reminder of why:

"We reject every shameful cover-up and refuse to resort to cunning trickery or distorting the Word of God. Instead, we open up our souls to you by presenting the truth to everyone's conscience in the sight and presence of God."

Later in the chapter it says that Jesus is revealed through our humanity. More permission, more grace over what was seemingly an error. I was the error.

I love the day I was able to connect this concept of being crushed but not killed. Crushed beyond what seems fair but look at me now. I'm still here. I'm making progress. I'm moving and breathing and continuing to learn and I am proud of how hard I have fought to have a life worth talking about. I haven't done a single fancy thing, but I know deeply that God is for me and that feels worth talking about. If He thinks He can make something in my life useful, then by all means have at it!

Somewhere in the beginning of the process, I remembered this curiosity I had toward kintsugi and decided on an impulsive whim to find someone who could show me. So even though it's a rare form of art, mostly mastered in Japan, I decided to give it a quick search. "Hey Siri, is there a kintsugi artist in Anderson, SC?" I miraculously found the one person who was local and used the art form. She incorporated gold into her paintings, and it was exquisite. Kintsugi traditionally is taken from broken ceramics that could be thrown in the trash and seen without value; a master artist will use gold to restore them, creating a deeper beauty than was there before.

Dionne White and I met for coffee, and I was on cloud nine at the glory of it all, a divine intervention. Dionne gave so much more than ideas about restoring things with gold. She helped me walk through prayer, releasing lies and soul ties. She's the one who told me I'm already whole, without scars, complete, and beautifully restored better than before with gold. She shared her story with such ease and grace. So many people have been instrumental in my progress. It's astoundingly beautiful to consider how each person's story helped me develop. Some definitely feel hand-picked for me.

2 Corinthians 4:6 (TPT)
Let brilliant light shine out of darkness.

In the spirit of creating something new and being authentic came my podcast. I had joined an online coaching program about taking action on your passion, whatever that means uniquely for you. It really served as permission to pursue boldly who I wanted to be, aligning my actions with my hopes. So the *Ash & Ivy Show* was born—and changed titles to *Stop Pretending* a year later—as a place to bring God close through story. Story makes God tangible. Each person's life reintroduces us to the Father in a unique way and encourages us to keep pursuing life. Seeing God in others pulls us awake!

Look in the face of any human and see the depths of story and beauty there. *Imago Dei* represented in hundreds of tiny and big ways. The podcast was definitely where I walked out my healing and found my voice. Telling the truth is so incredibly healing for the listener but I love the secret gift that telling the story gives the teller: hearing your own voice tell your own story is *the most powerful form of the Gospel!* It shows you God in you! There is absolutely nothing better than this because you can't argue it. It's evident. God is evident. Love is evident and it is for you.

The show was absolutely the thing that brought me to life. It was a small sacred space that allowed me to put language to my thoughts. It was a space to share. It was a space to grow confident and appreciate beautiful things, beautiful people. I was so inspired all of the time.

Hello idol.

Then, at 100 episodes and 10,000 downloads, I knew it was time to stop. I argued and resisted and felt very attached to this thing I had created from nothing. I thought it was the reflection of progress that I needed. It was so genuine and in line with what God had for me, but at the time my family needs were changing and I knew that it was time to shift again. I finally said my goodbyes and see you soons and committed to my family first. (I definitely have dreams for more podcasting!)

I quickly began to see more clearly where God was helping me make space to write, because the whole time I was hosting the show, that was the deepest longing of my heart. I really wanted it and that desire was growing, but I legitimately didn't have the time for it. In the most bizarre way, it was the most hidden piece of me. I tried to get to a writing conference one time and when I told my parents, who know me better than anyone, they were both surprised and confused. Separately, but in a unified response, "Writing?!" It was one of those big red flags that I wasn't living in alignment.

So gracious and kind Father helped me make space to do what was really in my heart to do, despite my protests to keep busy producing. My favorite moments on the podcast every single time were the conversations after I stopped recording. They were the best! So rich and true and deep. More times than I can count the person on the Zoom with me, out of the blue with nothing seemingly elicited by me, would say, "You should write a book."

And it felt like a jolt of lightning igniting what my heart already knew.

At that time, I didn't think it possible, and it felt way out of reach, but words spark life. That's why we tell. That's why we share and connect in authenticity so we can speak into each other's lives. Every single person has a story to share and is a reflection of their Maker and there is literally nothing more sacred than that. Jesus in you is such a miracle, and I definitely learned that I want to treat every single person with that knowing that Jesus is in them at the front of my mind.

Loving each person, sin and all, is ministering to Jesus himself.

Take a break from all the plans that you have made
And sit at home alone and wait for God to whisper
Beg him please to open up his mouth and speak
And pray for real upon your knees until they blister
Shine the light on every corner of your life
Until the pride and lust and slides are in the open
Then read the word and put to test the things you've heard
until your heart and soul are stirred and rocked and broken

Jimmy Needham, Clear the Stage

12
About Doubt

Two years of storytelling on the podcast developed a firm idea about what it means to seek the Lord. Jesus tells me to do very little: Love him completely, come to Him with my burdens, seek Him first. Well, what am I seeking and is this a game? I'm pretty sure my little boy is the best hider in a game of hide-and-seek. He hides to not be found! He hides a lot. He hides when we aren't seeking. He hides in department stores, grocery stores, farmers markets, and neighbors' houses. To be honest, many times I didn't even look for him. I just got tired of looking at some point and quit. I just assumed, hoped at best, he would come out eventually and all would be well.

One time, at least one time, I didn't look and he didn't come and he was really lost. Parenting wins for sure! But God, He tells me to seek. Does that mean He's hiding? Because I don't really feel like playing games. I mean, if you want to talk, then talk. If you want me to talk to you, then show up. Not to be demanding but what does seek mean? How do I seek someone who isn't there? How do we see someone who is invisible? How do we talk to someone who doesn't talk back? He is hidden for sure, but not hiding to withhold Himself. It's more like the screen tricks. Do you see black or blue? Does the image show an old lady's face or a young girl? Once you learn to see, you can't unsee, but until you find it, it seems hidden. Is it hidden by confusion, distraction, or busyness? Is it a fault of my own doing? By the way, my kid was found and it didn't change his tenacity to hide one bit, though he'll tell the story with full drama.

My oldest is now a teenager. As he grows, I feel this urgency to make sure I taught him every truth, even as I feel I am just starting to grasp them. I want him to have the fundamentals solid, unwavering. I want him to be confident and strong in any situation. I want him to know that he belongs and has everything within him to conquer every evil. I want him to have the depth of courage it requires to step into the unknown and create from nothing. My heart literally beats in my chest with ferocity for him to live a life of substance and thrill and adventure. But this seek and find life has to start with questions. If I could will him into a bright future I surely would. The truth is, for those things I long for to be true, my son must seek and find on his own. Because the real thrill of life is in the finding. I was never meant to be his savior and if I give it all to him to the very best of my ability, that will still never compare to his personal discovery of God's presence and voice and the depths of His love found in the Kingdom realm.

1 Corinthians 1:6 (TPT)
For the reality of the truth of Christ is seen among you and strengthened through *your experience* of him.

For so long I wanted to be that girl I followed or listened to or saw from afar who loved God big and was used big by Him. In my mind He picked her, like a teacher's pet. Why wasn't I ever good enough to be that person? People would say things like "God promised me this or God blessed me." So I spent years praying for God to use me in a big way, speak to me, tell me a good idea, and promise *me* something. Crickets. I am on my own. The book we studied in that first women's morning book club, the one I was so terrified about, was called *When Life and Beliefs Collide*. I figured we might as well dig deep if we were going to do it at all. It definitely had a crafty way of extracting the red flags of your heart. "Anger is a symptom not of how wrong God has gotten things but of our need to know him better" (pg. 65).

One day I was running on a trail through the woods when the roots of a tree caught my attention. I slowed my run, came to a stop actually, to really take in the details of these roots. The way they curved over the edge of the ravine where a creek bed rushed through captivated me and spoke to me a message of depth and hope. I had spent so much stupid energy pursuing the visible but I was learning to put my energy into the roots—good, strong, beautiful roots that dig deep and allow the tree to stand firm and grow gorgeous above reaching for the sun.

Suddenly as I was staring, panting out of breath, I realized God was letting me know, "*That's me. That's my voice for you.*"

Huh?! Why I had never put it together before was absolutely beyond me at that point. It felt dumb. I had loved God and listened to Him for a long time. I had obeyed His voice on many occasions. Life never gets old... usually I just need to learn the same darn lessons over and over on repeat. God's job has been pretty easy with this girl. Genuinely, in that moment connecting that creative flow, and the ever-present desire to use those thoughts to teach a concept, with the voice of my Creator completely changed my life.

The whole time I had been waiting for God to sound the way He sounds to *her*. I was watching for Him to tell me something He told someone else in a way He told *them*, as if I could guess what that was. Who God is and isn't to someone else is all make-believe in my head. Regardless, I had made God one thing in my head assuming He hated me and would never tell me anything important. I was failing to see that He talked to me CONSTANTLY! He was giving me cool thoughts, flowing in creativity, and that was Him reflected in me. That was His voice. That was unique for me. Wait. So I had been thinking He never talked to me but actually He talked to me all the time. In fact, He won't leave me alone. He is in all things, all thoughts, all plans. He is ever-present. Ever giving hope, ever helping me see with a new perspective. Ever filling with love. Because it can't be helped. The Maker makes Himself known.

> The Maker makes Himself known.

John 14:6-7 TPT

No one comes next to the Father except through union with me.
To know me is to know my Father too. And from now on you will
realize that you have seen him and experienced him.

I will realize I've already seen Him and experienced Him? So
when He says to seek Him, maybe that could mean, look for where
He was already there?

It is promised—even to me. But also to every person. I long to
know God is pursuing others. I want to get on the inside and
understand how it works. What it sounds like. How does He make
Himself known to someone in Japan? California? In poverty? How
does He lean down and whisper in the language of the one? He
does. Whether surfer, musician, gardener, or gang member...
Jesus knows how to speak the language. This is by far my favorite
thing about Him: the way He leans down, to be known, because
He knows you. I love that He speaks in a whisper so only you can
hear. It's sacred, just for you. I doubt it over and over that He
speaks, that He makes Himself known, but every time I start to
look again, I find it in every detail.

Unless you have a question, which unfortunately stems from
some kind of adverse event, pain, suffering, loss, hurt, you won't go
seek. Doubt is healthy. Doubt is a question longing to be
answered. Doubt might even be—you could dare to say—God
awakening you with an invitation to look for truth, to look for Him.
It seems fair enough to say we are all on a hunt for purpose and
meaning. There are endless books about finding oneself. Life
settles a bit when purpose is nestled comfortably within an easy
pursuit of abiding and connecting with God. All else flows from
this place with joy, peace, moments for patience and enduring,
naturally.

What I am here to say is that He wants to be found. He offers
mystery and depths that are immeasurable. You can look for years
and continue to be mesmerized by His grace. You can find Him in
every person. In every story. In every loss there is new life. In every

regret there is restoration. He is a God of creation, actively creating.

Doubt is the best thing we can have because it is a tool to propel us into the more God offers.

It is scary to have doubt. It almost feels wrong and secretive. We want to feel secure and steady. We want to know our boundaries and where to stop and where to return when things get rocky.

My doubt caught me by surprise. I had never before questioned the existence of God. Believing Him had always been simple until my aunt didn't get healed from cancer. I stood beside her in church, her hands raised in supernatural strength, as her body grew weary of the fight. That strength must have come from a deep desire to live. A deep desire to know the One who held her steady. Her safe place. I have a chalkboard she wrote a verse on: "But you, LORD, are a shield around me, my glory, the One who lifts my head high". I thought it was about being strong but now I know it was equally about the unspoken doubt, because as visible as God can be, He is very much invisible and often silent. Again and again we put our trust in the One. When you have no control over the outcome, you have no choice but to trust something. God is the only one who has any control. It's more than a last resort. Honestly, it takes immense courage to let go of the outcome and be in the present knowing the One who cares is in fact very near.

As I learned to face my doubt, realize my uncertainty, and be honest about it, then I started to ask God about it. I started to see that others had doubts too. How do you think all these books got written? They started with questions!

One of my favorite treasures in the Bible is when the disciples are with Jesus and He leads them to a quiet place away from the crowds and He takes time to explain what He meant. This tells me when I draw near to Him one-on-one, I am going to understand so much more and how it applies to me. I can lay love over my life and ask God what He has for me here. God isn't trying hard to be hidden; rather, He invites me into the hidden place so that the words given are for me, full of power and wonder. It isn't a mass message, it is for me only. We are chosen and known deeply. Let doubt lead me to that treasure every time. It is worth walking in the dark to find.

The sound that shakes the heavens
The whisper on the wind
Breaks my inhibitions
And settles me within
The mystery
You're closer than my skin
Your still, small voice
Moving me again
I hang on to every word You say
I live to hear You say my name
Speak to me

Kari Jobe, Speak to Me

13
Church Hurt

My whole long life of eighteen years, we had one couch. One everything really. One toast pan, too. It was small, probably the size of a sheet of paper, and pure black, burnt to a crisp, turning up on the edges as if it were becoming the thing it toasted all those years. We never even took it from the oven. Maybe we didn't even wash it. It had one job and it was perfect for it.

Our milk-chocolate-brown couch was a sectional with the deepest, comfiest cushions you can imagine, with lines like corduroy, that you could sink into for a long afternoon nap with my daddy; also perfect for flips and wrestling. My dad would pin me down with my arms raised above my head, "Who's got a question?" tickling my armpits, making me laugh until my stomach hurt. I'd yell out, "Stop!" and, "Don't!" and he'd laugh, "Don't stop?!" My dad was a captain in the United States Air Force. He came home in boots and camo every day of my life, unless he was deployed and then he didn't come home for weeks or months at a time. Every time my dad got stationed in a new place, the couch moved with us over and over, house to house.

Once my mom and then my dad chose to follow Jesus, everything changed in our house. Instead of hosting wild parties, that couch welcomed my dad for early mornings, dressed in his burgundy robe, Bible open, starting his day listening to Kenneth Copeland. Rated-R movies ended but of course nightly Wheel of Fortune and Jeopardy remained. I fell in love with the church in this season. With all those changes at home, my brother and I were also immersed into a church life we had never experienced before. Gone were the days of Sundays at the dirt bike track. Every Wednesday and Sunday we were with our church family, then we added in another night for band practice or Bible study. My parents don't do anything halfway.

That's where I met Mrs. Janice. She was the first person I ever knew who felt like love. I mean, when I think of her, I feel warmth through my body. She was genuine, caring and generous. She taught my Sunday school class and took all us middle school girls on a trip to her beach house. We got keepsake daiquiri glasses from the local seafood restaurant. For this girl whose main vacations were visiting grandma, it felt very grown up and fancy! She showed me who Jesus was for the first time and I chose to follow Him in the front row of that big, weird church where everyone clapped and hollered and danced. There were banners and cow bells. "Celebrate Jesus Celebrate" was on the weekly song rotation. It was safe, it was a place for me to belong. I made amazing friends. I was nicknamed Tigger and my friend was Pooh.

I love the church deeply. It was such a place of rescue for our family. When we started going to church, it wasn't the big fancy one on the corner with a steeple. It was usually the strangest one we could find. Don't ask me why, but my parents would just go down the Yellow Pages waiting on a feeling and then we would try it out! Literally so brave.

So when I wasn't living with my parents anymore, somehow I ended up at the fancy church, which took some getting used to, especially when the staff showed up at my door unannounced, came in uninvited, and questioned my baptism, as if their water was better than the rest. Though it may sound like I have some bitterness, I really don't. It was enlightening to the ways of their tradition and opened my perspective to see differently, to see better. The treasures I found there served me with great significance. The greatest treasures were the women, more specifically, each woman, one at a time.

Rarely when we hear the heart of one can we stay in a place of judgment. Sure, a collective group may carry a message that doesn't seem to be a perfect fit, and there is a right place for assessing those things and following the Lord to make your best decision. This was more about the recognition that even in places that don't necessarily align with one way of thinking, there are individuals who reflect the image of the Creator who is Rescuer for all.

I fell in love with the women and leadership of that church and am eternally grateful for that opportunity. I was welcomed into homes and Bible studies. I was loved sincerely and deeply. Some differences just aren't worth battling over because at the end of the day, God is enough for us all. He is the one who knows how to lean in and speak to the heart of the one, and I believe He is indeed doing that for each person, no matter if they are following the strictest of traditions or aren't following anything at all.

Recently, a homeless woman in our church was sharing with me parts of her story and I just laughed so much at it. Growing up, her dad was a Pentecostal minister, and he would always tell her, "You can jump all you want but when you hit the ground, walk straight." Honestly, God is capable of speaking and meeting you no matter what you're doing—walking, jumping, or sleeping. He is the one who pursues and draws every heart. He is the faithful one. More than ever in my life do I trust this to be true.

We spend so much energy focused on details that fade. We need to fix our eyes on Jesus. The gospel is the same for all of us. For some, my depiction of God and Him speaking to me may seem mystical. I could be making private things too public, but if the gospel isn't personal then what even is the point? To me, even church is just an extension of the very personal daily connection with things we can't see. It is a place to come together with others who get that, who can talk about it without feeling weird. Not to the exclusion of others, but it's a place to belong and maybe be understood, at least a little bit.

Telling the Truth, by Frederick Beuchner, gives a brilliant illustration of the gospel as tragedy, comedy and fairytale.

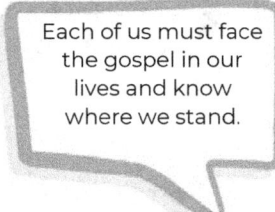
Each of us must face the gospel in our lives and know where we stand.

Regardless of our differences in how we approach God or view water or presence or song, ultimately, each of us must face the gospel in our lives and know where we stand. So in my words, and some of Beuchner's, the gospel must start as bad news. Eventually we are unmasked, stripped bare of the clothes that hide the real parts of us, but we know they are there. Then to make it a comedy, the gospel gives the unexpected. With God we are "loved anyway, cherished, forgiven, bleeding to be sure, but also bled for. That is the comedy, and yet, so what? So what if even in his sin, the slob is loved and forgiven when the very mark and substance of his sin and and of his slobbery is that he keeps turning down the love and forgiveness because he either doesn't believe them or doesn't want them or just doesn't give a damn?" (pg. 7). Beuchner goes on to assure that the gospel ends in fairy tale. For every dark there is light. For every broken thing there is redemption and for every thing lost it is found in Him who holds the world in his hand. "Just as in fairy tales extraordinary things happen." God does outlandish things and usually in a darkness that is soon to swallow us whole. He makes impossible things possible!

I love this line: "Rich or poor, successes or failures as the world counts it, they are the ones who are willing to believe in miracles because they know it will take a miracle to fill the empty place inside them where grace and peace belong with grace and peace."

What emptiness in your life was filled by miracle? This is gospel in your life and essential to experiencing Jesus. The gospel laid over your own story will bring life: something from nothing. A baby filling your womb. A friend filling a hole. A creative outlet to fill a need. Miracle on miracle is God's love for me. It's comedy over tragedy. The most extraordinary piece of this concept is that so much of the time we don't even see the comedy happening while in our rebellion. We are all in our feelings and drowning in our humanity while God is working miracles. It's only when we look back we can finally see without the fog of survival that despite the pain there was beauty. Despite our choices, our doubts, or failings, God was faithful and good to make a way.

To my oldest son's absolute delight, comedy and fairy tale came in one when we welcomed our second baby boy into the world amidst big hard things. He was comic relief and has been every day since, though much of the time he is also the cause of the need for comic relief! We weren't clear on his name until after his birth, with a room full of visitors, his dad and I texted each other using subtle discretion in order to make a final decision. We knew his name had to be Keean, "gift from God". He's the gift that gives and gives and gives and we're asking God, "What do you want me to do with all this giving?" He is teaching me, challenging me, and sending me to prayer on the daily. He is the pure image of delight, enthusiasm and dogmatism. His zeal for life is most contagious and we absolutely need him in our family. My favorite thing about Keean is his ability to see in the brightest colors. Every story he tells is lavished in bigger and better details, but I've come to realize he really sees it that way!

Isn't everything pushing us to ask God questions? "God, what do you have for me in this? Where is the gospel in this? What is good? What do I focus on?"

My life is my cross to bear, my story, my very tangible reality. Take it up, look at it, examine it, know it, feel the feelings, and give it with a rawness that requires trust that someone good will receive it.

I guess I've decided the truth is worth telling. To the best of my ability. There is a song I sing to my kids when I'm rubbing their heads to sleep. It includes this precious comforting line, "I want to lay my head back and feel your heartbeat." With so much division I find myself longing for this rest, just a closeness that isn't hindered by controversy, but a simple trust that He is enough. As I write words that pierce the deepest parts of my soul, I pour them out in worship, and go back to what I know to be true. He grounds me, He fills me with life, He is my safe place.

When the church is being criticized, which is always at this point, I hide in the cleft and let His whisper find me. I know that the church and Jesus are not the same, but it still feels hard to hear such harsh hate toward people in either direction. The gospel is secure. We can lay it over any topic and it will hold true. Racial division, abortion, women's rights, sexual identities, immigration, poverty, or war. The gospel does not bend to these, though we ask where is the fairy tale in some of these places? Sometimes love is hard to find and sometimes we look back into our stories and in certain things we don't find it at all. The gospel reaches beyond the things we can see and penetrates the heart. It takes the very worst things and invites us beyond what we can see into what is safe eternally.

I want the church to be that safe place. I want the church to rise up as a place of generous love, a love that gives identity and burns with compassion. A place that radically calls each of us into the people we are designed to be, invites us higher, makes space for us to see with clarity. A place that securely and boldly loves, its own identity unthreatened by the complexity of humanity. It hurts my heart when I hear believers speaking poorly of the church and worse, walking away. Why is there so much church hurt? Is it our expectations? Is it false teaching? I can't believe it is intentional for the church to cause hurt, but that is through rose-colored lenses, I'm aware. Churches all over America are teaching many many things against the pure purpose of connecting with God and others; intentional or not, it is wrong. If not leading to greater connection and reflecting His image, the rest is a waste.

Abiding securely in a relationship with our Father, as sons and daughters, completely immersed in His full love, should be the main agenda of the church, of each one building the body of the church. This agenda must be initiated by each individual. We have a space where we belong and are made whole. If we spent all of our energy focused on believing that God's love is big enough to cover, that His desire is for me to find Him, that He literally chases me down to give me the truth, how powerful could our lives be? Only glory can flow from that. That is a real place of rest. That is a place where peace resides. Truth can only produce fruit. It is the essence of freedom. When we tell our stories, it sheds light over all our "life facts" and lets freedom give us belonging—allowing in comfort to mend the hurt.

Look closely: each life within the church, and without, holds an immense story that reflects grace. Knowing people individually, when you really hear someone and see their lives, you can't help but bend with compassion toward them. This goes in all directions. We need more compassion for each other. That doesn't solve all the problems and it is likely an ignorant stance. Nonetheless, it is mine. I just wonder what kind of people we could be if we spent less energy on symptoms and instead encouraged people in prophecy and who God says they are. Speak it into existence, the language of Heaven.

Love is in highest demand. It is time for the church, for each person who builds the church, to seek God in his and her own life and walk in healing to spread the fragrance of God everywhere.

I attended youth group during the True Love Waits era. We attended big conferences and had small groups and read books all about waiting until marriage for the big act. There was an incredibly admirable older high school girl who spoke to the youth group one time. Our small group of probably twenty-five high school kids sat on the bleachers, I'm sure acting thoroughly obnoxious, while she paced the gym floor telling her story and her love for God. Of course, this boldness and courage resonated with me. She was beautiful and funny and happy. I remember when I heard that she got pregnant how shocked I was. Even perfect funny people who love God break, fall short of expectations. I can't help but wonder if the push for True Love Waits and the complete emphasis on sexual purity being the most important detail of Christianity as a youth could have limited my perspective as to what the actual point of Christianity was about. There were two main agendas: True Love Waits and Have Your Quiet Time. Okay, got it. Wait, what if that doesn't work? Then what? I was thirty-five before I believed I wasn't failing when I didn't have my quiet time.

I do believe that marriage is God's design for coming together as one, physically, mentally, and spiritually. Marriage models sacrificial love in the rawest display of intimacy. Anyone who has tried it knows full well that romance isn't the top and only agenda of marriage. Rather it is a stripping of self that can happen in no other context, because you are fully exposed, unable to hide weakness. Vulnerability made mandatory for true intimacy. Supernatural strength is required for the daily doses of forgiveness and laying down oneself to reach a place of being known and knowing.

My husband and I are eighteen years in and have hardly scratched the surface of what this means. How do you fully know someone? Geez, we are just beginning to know ourselves well enough to talk about it. Choosing one person again and again and again and more so to be loved like that in return is a daily miracle. Jesus gives us this example of loving deeply all while knowing the truth of a person. It feels impossible for us to grasp and we repeatedly strive to mask our imperfections, making ourselves look and feel presentable, even to our spouse. At least that's what I do. I want to impress him!

I have a golden ring: three roped bands welded together tightly unified, not unlike the trinity. It was given to me by my parents when I was 15. I was directed to sit down on the brown sectional, sinking in deeply. I wasn't able to really sit formally, because it was sagging with age, even though I could tell this conversation was important. I'm pretty sure my dad sat on the L of the couch and my mom just sat right in front of me on the coffee table. "Let's talk."

I honor my parents for taking time and thoughtfulness to have this conversation with me, I think this conversation was essential. Of course, we want our children to be safe, to be loved, to understand the depths of impact their decisions make. It's not that different from that well intended program of my youth. Its very pure goal was to save all those kids from the destruction caused by giving your heart away without considering the very real consequences. Doing things against God's way can have widespread consequence.

As a teenager, I think I must have thought all my actions happened in a vacuum: that none of them carried consequence into my adult life. I was still a kid for crying out loud! What I couldn't see was past that season of impulsivity and narrow thinking was a whole entire life. It's like a game called Blokus. It has geometrical-shaped pieces, like Tetris, but you play on a flat board, with confined borders, limiting your spaces. The goal is to fit all your pieces in efficiently, connecting them by a tip, avoiding interference of the opposing players. If you make a mistake early on, there are more options. Every decision impacts the next. Nothing is done in isolation. Nothing is without impact. This can create a definite fear agenda but ultimately you just have to keep moving.

I just wish the ring and the book and all the hoopla could have saved me. Despite all their effort, my heartache wasn't prevented. Maybe our agendas for the youth need to be centered on ways to establish genuine relationships with Jesus in a way that fosters holiness, awe of who He is, and a love for Him because we know His character. Even then, in authentic response to His grandness, we will inevitably fall and maybe it would be helpful to let the kids know in advance that it is going to be okay.

In 1999, as a senior in high school, my journal lacked depth or foresight, but I jotted down this note on scratch paper and somehow it got saved: "I catch myself yearning for more of what I see in others. I need to not be envious of those things that are not of God. I should make sure I am following perfection."

I quoted Psalm 37:1 (NIV) which reads:

"Do not fret because of those who are evil or be envious of those who do wrong."

So while that is noteworthy, in high school and equally at forty years of age, the line of my own hand about following perfection is likely a good indication of my sideways theology. There is a difference in striving for perfection vs. a latter thought at verse 5:

"Give God the right to direct your life and as you trust him along the way you'll find he pulled it off perfectly!"

It doesn't ever say: "*You will be perfect so exhaust yourself with this effort and if you fail, which you will, you'll be worthless.*" For this point, I like the use of the word *perfectly* in The Passion Trasnlation. While we know the words it *does* say are true, if we're honest and paying attention, we will catch our heart actually believing they aren't. What we think we believe versus what we actively practice thinking are likely two very different things.

When I moved home and integrated into the singles group at my parents' church, there was definite judgment when they realized I was the "D" word. Don't worry, I didn't stay in the singles group long anyways!

I've been in many conversations with church people about other people and their decisions, usually highlighting their "Ooh she did what?!" moments, mainly for the sake of juicy conversation. We hyper analyze the conditions people face instead of seeing their name written in the book of life and recognizing that God is able to take every single piece of who they are to create life.

I wonder how I would have processed differently if someone had spoken words of a future and life to me. I wish I could hear the conversations I know are happening all over where people are speaking life into someone else, reminding them that mistakes aren't their story! Sometimes it feels like all I hear is judgment. Judgment about what she's wearing, judgment about if he's gay or not, or did she get pregnant on her honeymoon. Judgment is always paired with a lack of humility and results in a lost relationship. When we judge someone or assume details about their lives or draw conclusions about who they are, more likely than not, we are not going to also dig in to know their soul, understand their pain, and offer a healing hand or just friendship. I am at the top of this guilty list.

That was a point in my life where I really struggled to know who I was. '*Am I who I thought? I know who I want to be, who I try to be, but people only see my stupidity. What must they think?*' And I quickly stuffed that inconsistency of my character away and made it invisible, because I didn't know what else to do with it. '*I better get back to being what I know is secure and acceptable.*'

Was I the girl who loved Jesus with her entire being, longing to do amazing things for Him, love Him well, change the world for Him?

Or was I the girl who chose boys over friends, was late for curfew, and gave up all her dreams for nothing?

It's not so unrelatable today. Am I the girl who loves Jesus wholeheartedly and will lay down my image in order to share His life-giving love?

Or am I the girl who keeps one foot in both places, striving to fit in, and be normal enough to be accepted and likable?

Understanding this dynamic complexity of humanity while holding Christianity is immensely difficult. We want to blame something or someone tangible. It's the church, it's the pastor, it's that Christian who is such a hypocrite. Perfection shouldn't be our goal in the first place. We can only attach to things we feel some control over. Then we try to assert that control over others, as if their sin might rub off on us or our children. Sin doesn't taint the name of Jesus. Sin is rampant out "in the world" and in our own homes. Jesus is not afraid of sin. In fact, in every single story, Jesus moves toward it! Hugging the person, pushing away those who condemn. Jesus sees beyond sin.

Is my voice getting louder? Absolutely. There is no bigger message than this. Our focus is in the wrong place. We are missing the entirety of God's truth when we focus only on right and wrong. Yes, He calls us to purity and no we shouldn't live our lives drowning in sin, because this steals our hopes and future, but the paradox is that when we focus on love, his unfailing ocean-deep love, allowing it to engulf our insecurities filling our need for grace and fresh air, all the details of sin fade. They don't win the attention!

In this place we can believe He is enough. He absorbed every ounce of judgment on the cross and left it in the grave. He is enough. Breathe in peace right here and now. It is mine fully and it is yours. We are known fully, loved fully,

> He absorbed every ounce of judgment on the cross and left it in the grave. He is enough.

and fully whole in Jesus Christ. This is what builds the body of Christ. Tragically beautiful people who have practiced surrender, exchanging their shame and fears for the love of God, who have been forgiven much, are most able to look at their neighbor and see the heart that God sees. Not seeing their condition, not confining them to their errors or calling them dirty, but raising them up to who they truly are.

Jesus, help me be this person.

Shame shrank me as a person hiding me behind a shield of self-protection because there is a very real enemy stealing any hope, stealing my voice of resurrection. I know that in all those years of putting on my happy face and working to impress my pastor, I never once felt like he was proud of me. We hung out with them. We were "liked" and included, but it never felt like enough. Is that the pastor's fault? No. Shame had a very sneaky way of guarding me. To keep myself safe, I didn't let myself be entirely known. I didn't feel good enough and so I played small. I only point out the pastor because I think I want so much to belong on that level. I long to be able to teach others about who Jesus is.

So there is a cyclical war at play. Yes, humans are involved and they probably don't always do the best thing in someone else's interest. Moreso, I didn't believe I was loved therefore I simply couldn't love well or be loved well. So much energy is spent dealing with these things in isolation. It is so anti-fun to bring down the vibe and tell how you feel. My voice was mute, silenced from helping others. I was social but isolated, making my connections limited. It's easy to sink into thinking that we are alone in our struggle. That line of thinking resulted in me hiding and keeping my freedom and what God had done to myself.

What it really does is keep God small, unapproachable, and out of reach. Telling the truth of our weakness and need for grace shows life and possibility. It brings heaven to earth and shows us the way to a very real, personable, generous God. We cannot know the hurt of another unless we are willing to give of ourselves. Know someone and you will know their hurt. Nothing less than compassion can result. Part of getting to know my own story was doing this very thing for myself. I had to seek healing and find love in my own story, I had to experience God's favor and voice and covering for myself. I had to know deep in my bones that He is for me and completely shed myself of a need for pastoral approval or parental approval or friend approval. My identity is shaped only by a deep ever-present love that exists in my marrow. In my soul. It is steady and safe.

Only then could I know the depth of my sin and still believe I am fully loved and worthy. I am whole.

Cause You are closer, closer than my skin
And you are in the air I'm breathing in
And here's where the dead things come back to living
I feel my heart beating again
It feels so good to know You are my friend

This is where I'm meant to be
Me in You, and You in me
I don't have to prove a thing
You're already approved of me

Maverick City Music, Communion

14

Another Drive

Driving is so exhilarating and a great space for quality time with myself. Rarely in any other setting am I trapped in one spot for more than an hour to be with my thoughts. I love the speed and the independence. One of my favorite parts of going to college in Orlando was the long interstate drives home. As a mom with minimal experience with that feeling in years, I crave that open road feeling. The trips for these interviews did not go wasted. Just as much life-changing impact happened in the car as it did in the houses.

On this particular trip, I was driving toward the center of our state blaring 2020's best worship. Probably "Reckless Love" and "Do it Again" or "Quiet" by Elevation Worship and "Speak to Me" by Kari Jobe. Just fully immersed in a time of pouring out my heart in earnest worship and prayer. And really what I mean by those fancy Christian words is I was frustrated by my life and my regrets and I didn't want to do what I was about to do out of sheer terror. Was I going to swim with a wild monster? Nope, just going to see my best friend of a million years. The brain is strange, completely out of proportion, disillusioned. Why couldn't I just take a big breath, own my stuff, and say sorry and be done with it? Why all the emotion and fear?

So I was telling God emphatically how much I hated it all.

I hate my story.

I hate doing this.

I have no friends.

I don't want to talk about it.

You know how things spiral when you're pouting.

132

I hate it.

I don't want to face rejection.

I don't want someone to be mad at me and tell me how horrible I am. I much prefer to be liked and adored. I like to impress people, not disappoint them.

God, don't make me go!

More words out of the blue, amidst my angst:

Riley, that is not your story. I AM your story.

I'm not saying it was audible, but it was very clear. A new thought. A new perspective. A brand new storyline, not of my own head. My anguished line enveloped in a one liner of love. It was complete. If shame and torture and humiliation and rejection and disappointment aren't my story, what is? How can those not be my story anymore? Don't I just need to own it and wear it well and suck it up and be responsible? Don't I need to suffer the consequences of my own choices and pay for what I did?

It is hard to put emphasis on this in a way that shows that this statement of I AM was like a blanket. Absolute. Without error. It hushed every competing voice or thought, memory or regret. Shhhhhh... peace and silence.

God didn't leave this one to a person. He didn't wait for the conversation. He handled it right then and there. He changed my narrative from hating my story to believing my story is the greatest gift of all because it is Him in me. Miracle on miracle. Every hour a gift.

Psalm 34:1-4 (TPT)

Lord! I am bursting with joy over what you've done for me! My lips are full of perpetual praise. I'm boasting of you and all your works, so let all who are discouraged take heart. Join me, everyone! Let's praise the Lord together. Let's make him famous! Let's make his name glorious to all. I cried to God in my distress, and he answered me. He freed me from all my fears!

Gaze upon him, join your life with his, and joy will come. Your faces will glisten with glory. You'll never wear that shame face again.

I don't want to break this sacred moment, but this is probably one of my top five Bible verses for more than one reason; I would be lying if I didn't say it's because that "shame-face" comment kills me! This is God's word, paraphrased in The Passion Translation, which is similar to The Message in that it is more of an emotive interpretation of one author, and not to be used in isolation without a true translation. I really enjoy the poetic language and find it to be encouraging to add expanding thought to familiar scriptures. This particular use of "shame-face" makes me immediately think of a current-ish slang term "Resting B Face", usually just called RBF, which will just have to be Googled. So many of us are stuck in our own heads! We are absorbed with our own thoughts and agendas and frankly it comes across as not very friendly. Listen, I spent a considerable amount of time trying to learn to cuss, but just failing. I do not cuss. Ever. I know that's really kind of lame. The coolest Christians these days at least whisper cuss. I don't know all the answers. Don't blame me. Still, this verse makes me laugh every time.

I used to teach a parenting class to women whose children were in the court system. One woman in particular captured my heart. Anita. She came into our class for the first time, so completely beat up. Just withdrawn and without hope. She looked tired and ashen in coloring. I have documented in my journal how her appearance radically changed throughout the class. She was filled with joy, she smiled and grew in confidence and awe of life. The most remarkable difference was how her skin completely changed! She came to life! She attached her identity to being a daughter of God, no longer lost and alone, but having a place to belong, loved fully. Just like me in that car. Changed. When my story was covered by His story of grace and love, I knew I wasn't the same either. I could look people in the eye with confidence, offering friendship and grace, in a way I couldn't risk before.

Spirit lead me where my trust is without borders
Let me walk upon the waters
Wherever You would call me
Take me deeper than my feet could ever wander
And my faith will be made stronger
In the presence of my Savior

Hillsong UNITED. Oceans

15
More to the Story

I always dreamed of having a lifelong friend, but I moved so much and friendships only lasted three years. I lived my life subconsciously thinking I would just make new ones and it's taken me forever to break that habit in order to commit to the longevity relationships require. I was literally always the third wheel. Everywhere I moved, I was liked and welcomed in but always to a group of friends already established. Of course, this was great and I can totally see the logic of it all. I could list all the sets off to prove I'm not being dramatic, but that's probably obnoxious. All I've ever wanted was to be someone's favorite. That would be a lot of pressure though wouldn't it? I'm not sure I am qualified. Actually I'm sure I am not.

I was fussing about friends in my head one time. Just straight-up whining about it. Then I started thinking about every friend I have collected through my constant moving and realized I have years of friendships from lots of places built. I was surprised by how very rich in friendship I am. In every season of my life, I've had what I needed. I wish I could name them all. Some have lasted and some have moved on and I've learned that is okay. Each friendship and the way it shaped me at the time of need is one to be cherished. I could gush over the vastness of it. When I lived away from home I felt really alone. I knew things weren't going well and it was hard to know who to tell. I had one friend who took me into her home and just let me be a part of her family. Love her!

At that same time, I signed up through our church to host a women's Bible study. Oddly, only one woman showed up: *the one*

I had heard had been through a previous marriage and the one who ended up mothering me over the next year. I still wonder what she must have thought when she arrived at this young girl's house, a stranger in this family church, and how this whole thing unfolded. God knew exactly how he would cover me in that season. Those two relationships saved me, literally saved me. It is treasures like these that I found as I dug through my story.

All through childhood, my life was full of friendship. It brings a huge smile on my face to think of them all. I rode my bike for miles, sometimes round and round and sometimes sneaking to a gas station with nickels and dimes for Laffy Taffy. In my imagination I can see myself flying down the neighborhood street, usually with no hands, friends joining in, coming and going happily and as they please and me just free with speed in my hair. I think if I picture freedom, it must be on that bike!

With too much freedom, I found myself shooting that guy in the knee with his BB gun or jumping off the barn onto the trampoline or breaking the back windshield of that friend's truck with a Coke bottle. Stories. Memories. Friendship. I gifted my beloved beta fish to another friend when we moved. It was the kind in a vase with a plant on top. Sounds silly but I had kept that thing alive for record time and I felt the loss. I attempted to help a friend insert her first tampon, not because I had ever seen one before, but because I was insistent she go with me to the waterpark. I spent the night with another girl and watched her mom worship in dance in the mornings. I always wished I were that unabandoned. She is also the friend who peed herself every time we were together because I always made her laugh to that point, even though she begged me not to! What is wrong with me?!

Friendship completely opens your world to possibility and fun. I just love it and am thankful for it. Having friendships as an adult remains really hard but I've managed to keep a few of the best.

Funny how friends come to be in unexpected ways. One of my best friends, Erica, with whom I know I will be friends forever, seemed to have found me. It was so backwards from my life pattern of moving into friendships, hence such a beautiful gift, because I didn't have to work for it or chase her! She and her husband picked our church because it had a basketball team. Isn't that so fun? Then she picked me as a friend! You never know what will welcome someone in! It feels good to be the one someone else wants as a friend. It started with our toddlers at the pool then growing up together on the soccer field. Through raising those toddlers into teenagers while growing up ourselves and working on our marriages, we've grown in deep and rich friendship. It's true through and through. She and a couple of other girls are the most incredible group of genuine friends that I could ask for. We all know marriage takes a lot of work but friendship as adults is a commitment rarely talked about! Sometimes months sneak by without us coming together but we love to celebrate one another, cheer for one another, and pray for one another. When we are together it is rich and nothing gives life quite like best friends.

In my years of figuring all this out, I would cave into myself, take breaks from it all, but these girls have always been there, loyal, available. Availability is a gift that is beyond anything else I used to think I needed in friendship. Erica has a gift of giving her time, her whole self, and it is a stunning gift. It's hard for me to match words with that kind of love. It's extremely rare and something I cherish more and more with age. I'm old enough now to have friends who have stood the test of time. I find myself learning that I don't need new ones every 3 years. I need to sow into the ones I have, planting depths and grace and beauty that is only found in something nourished.

Another friend in a long list, Stefini, absolutely made my dream come true for a "friend forever". When I never thought I would carry friendship from childhood into adulthood, because I didn't grow up in one place, Stefini showed me what is possible and has been there for it all! Even though we don't live near each other or even talk that much in our current busy seasons, when we are together I feel at home. She literally sees through me like a freaking superhero.

I say that but can also say that I was trembling when she was next on my list for a 'Rewrite Your Story' trip visit. Stupid scared. This girl is intimidating. She's got it together. Everything she does is intentional, and she is the epitome of good. With the birth of her first baby girl, she parented with the wisdom of a seasoned mother and exuded beautiful grace. I don't know how she does it.

One time I sat at her kitchen counter and gawked as she handled each person in her family with firm, commanding, beautiful, elegant ease. Everyone knew their role and job. She was respected by her kids and her husband adored her.

I felt like a blob next to her. That is so ugly to say, and speaking negatively about myself doesn't actually give her the compliment she deserves, because the truth is she is kind and extremely generous and she brings out the best in me. She always has time for whomever she is with. We can be together and somehow she can be completely listening to me and give her full attention to one of her four children or husband then as in a dance turn fully back to me with her huge smiling eyes. She's stunning, but that's how jealousy and shame work. It separates and isolates and builds walls and lies that keep people apart. Truth unites. Humility and transparency and connection unites. So fear and lies came between us because I was scared. I now see that lies and unforgiveness were preventing me from trusting her fully. They had grown larger in my mind than the very evident truth. I had rehearsed the wrong things and this made me forget what was real.

So Stefini and I met shortly after I became a Christian, in 8th grade, when we moved to her hometown of tiny Sumter, SC. She has been steadfast and wonderful ever since. She is strong and unmoving, seemingly without temptation, although I know now, also untrue. Though she has little tolerance for foolishness, she leans in close. She listens intently. She asks rich, true and deep questions. She is insightful and observant. I always feel like my best self when I am with her. I feel cherished and seen. I never feel judged... except that one time.

Let me start at the beginning.

In Sumter, I was well protected by my reputation for being the good girl. I was richly surrounded by Christian friends and their families. I was involved in youth group and the worship team. My school friends could say, "Don't ask Riley because she'll say no." My standards were high and my intentions were clear. Peer pressure was never a thing for me. I spent loads of time in the Bible learning and growing and only listening to Christian music, probably Avalon and Point of Grace. There my dreams came alive, as did my self-righteousness.

Stefini and I shared that time of growth together, with loads of fun, usually over a bag of salt and vinegar chips. I love this memory of us: In Sunday School we had this teacher—apparently who Stefini didn't care for—and I finally

I can't remember her at all!

interrupted this teacher to say, "You keep saying we know the story, but I didn't grow up in church and I don't know the story." She watched me grow and learn and establish my faith during those early high school years. When I moved home, many years later and with many scars, Stefini and I went to Charleston together and it was the best time I had had in a long time. I felt young and free again. I felt like me. I felt.... good.

More years later, on my 'Rewrite' journey, I showed up at her house and she knew the plan was for us to discuss my story, so she had carved out precious time for us to be together. The fact that people did this for me continues to astound me to this day. Connection is my favorite thing! So we had a couple of hours together to catch up on all the details, reminisce, and reconnect. It is such an awkward thing to just start talking about yourself. Who even does that? "Sit down, I need to talk about myself." Honestly, it's atrocious, yet these women who God directed me to made space for me and poured grace out lavishly. They gave me presence and time, and their attention alone restored my soul. I am so incredibly undeserving of any of it.

In my doubt about sharing, she said, "He wants you to share so you will see He was there." These were familiar words because I remembered they were exactly what I learned when I shared at the December ladies brunch and they were simply the essence of this whole mission. He was there. He had been there the whole time. "I will never leave you. I will carry you. You are held. Let's catch the foxes together." In every season He never left, always providing a way, always guiding.

Stefini was so kind to acknowledge my idealistic, full throttle spirit and gave grace that I could not have predicted. Living with a full glass perspective is nothing to apologize for, but we can all also acknowledge trouble has its place in that personality! Once I got through what I had intended to talk about, I took a deep breath and was relieved to be done and she said, "What do you think about what happened next?"

Clothed in rainbows of living color
Flashes of lightning rolls of thunder
Blessing and honor strength and glory and power be
To You the only one who's King

Kari Jobe

16

Babies Happen

When I told Stefini the news for the first time, I was driving down the interstate toward a bridal shop in Buckhead, a suburb of Atlanta, GA. I was working there as a behavior therapist and I got to "live" in a skyrise condo with a view of skyscrapers for five whole minutes. Check! Accomplished that scrapbook page.

So, when I called her to tell her I was pregnant, shortly after my unseemly divorce, I was all alone and felt even more so desolate. She screamed my name, completely exasperated and shocked. I thought she was mad and disappointed, but I think she was actually sad for me. I didn't blame her for being mad. I was wrong and I did disappoint her, but it still stung really badly.

My wedding dress didn't come from the shop in Buckhead or even from the Crew summer line. In fact, my mom kindly picked up the off-white dress with spaghetti straps at a thrift store, as if I were going to a school dance. It certainly lacked the linen flow of peace that could have clothed me in grace, but it fit and was $10 so that seemed to meet the standard at the time. It's not the kind of dress I would want my daughter to pretend in, in front of a mirror, and imagine herself as a bride fully loved and adored. Redeemed, there are many other things I want to pass on to her instead, so I won't stay in a sad spot about this.

My husband and I wed on Valentine's Day on the coast of Key West, FL, on a record cold shivering day with only us and our parents. My dad and Joshua got off the cruise ship early to scout out a perfect spot and ended up in the exact spot of our imaginations. Palm trees and all. Funny thing, they couldn't find a public beach anywhere but could see the perfect spot on a military base. Being retired Air Force, my dad decided to try his luck at the entrance gate. The guy working was divinely also retired Air Force and let us walk right in! During our ceremony, another couple walked up and chose to sit right beside our wedding ceremony placing their chairs directly between us and the water. Bizarre and hilarious, oblivious. My dad is super poetic and beautiful in moments like these, so he made a powerful speech about love, uniting us with a collection of sand from the sacred spot. Problem is, he forgot the portion of the vows where we repeat all of our promises. I think we covered it all in our own handwritten vows so we should be good to go, but just in case, "Joshua, I do!" It was simple and sacred and intimate and absolutely beautiful.

Big weddings are spectacular and fun and certainly a celebration worth having, but ultimately and for us in that moment what I needed it to be was him looking at only me and promising to hold tight forever. Unlike many other details of my story, this one I really really cherish. The sanctity of marriage is unlike any other bond, and I wanted to go locked in, clinging to one another above all.

Like all marriages, there have been really amazing times and there have been seasons of just holding on, for we've learned it will pass. Our marriage has been a slow discovery of how to be real with one another. I think we both just wanted success so badly, we were afraid to rock the boat, but it has blossomed into more and more of turning to each other in vulnerability and trust. Jesus, only Jesus.

Later that week, my dad, along with my new husband, tried their luck on the cruise ship dance floor and even got some dollar bills. Some things that happen on cruises, especially ones that you end up doing with your parents on your honeymoon, definitely need to stay on the cruise ship! This story just gets weirder and weirder.

Six months later, after thirty-two hours of labor, we welcomed our baby boy into the world.

Throughout the whole drawn-out labor and delivery ordeal, we had a room full of friends and family. They had become quite comfy on the green plastic couches, kindly offered for the laboring mom's fans, so much so they didn't even have on shoes. When they stepped out for what seemed like the millionth time so the one actually in labor, uncomfy in the bed, could be checked, they had no idea the re-entrance would be closed with their shoes locked inside. My doctor kindly said he would "let me try to push" as a peace offering, I think, before a C-section. Push I did, for an entire hour, until our boy found his way into a whirlwind of cold air and loud voices and extra IVs, earning an extra week in the hospital. I fought so incredibly hard for him that day and it was only the beginning of learning to fight for him in this chaotic world. The doctor called me a beast and that is a title I've recalled proudly on many occasions as I've learned to push through fights that I didn't really ask for.

No part of me or his dad regrets getting pregnant with him. He was absolutely the greatest gift of our lives. Not a single part of me wants a redo, because I love him with my entire being. I don't have words for the complexity of unexpected grace because a baby coming into the world as grace with skin is beyond my wildest imagination. There is not another love like this. A baby. A baby to soften hearts. A baby to unite families. This must be why Jesus came like this. Vulnerable and inviting. Without intimidation. Fragile and tender, teaching us what it means to be needy and receive. Teaching us the stillness of awe and wonder. A baby is how God chose to respond to my selfishness. Forever shattered is my heart for him. His dad and I united over our immense adoration for this new life.

So on my 'Rewrite' visit, as Stefini and I sat on her couch and she prompted this reflection by asking me what happened next, I smiled big. She's that kind of friend. Gentle plus truth. I told her no one else had asked me about that and how much I appreciate it; however, I had not really prepared. I hadn't thought about it much. What I had thought about in my new state of mind was how I wanted to remember it well. I wanted to see the good. I wanted to see and tell of the Lord's goodness. I didn't want to feel ashamed. I didn't want to keep it a secret.

While that sentiment is very true and possible by God's design for me to walk whole and restored, it isn't as easy as just deciding. As I unraveled the details of this part of my story, I realized the exact lie that needed to be replaced. I got the largest lump in my throat and raw feelings spilled forth, unexpected. Sharing about this grief of ruining my second chance felt complex. It was "my Christian image", charred again. It was my goal renewed to do something useful and good, instead of serving myself, gone again. It was the devastation of bringing someone else down with me. Feelings of sorrow for my husband who accepted all of me and loved me in my numbness; he was unwavering. To get pregnant stole so many things from him that seemed really important, like a bachelor's weekend. Groomsmen. Let me get honest, it was not only being pregnant, it was this being my second wedding. We lost the grand setting. Me in a big white dress. All the love from friends and family that comes with a wedding. There was a hole where these things were meant to be. He did have precious friends help us celebrate with a luau reception and we absolutely cherish that memory. Stefini listened through all of my processing then spoke truth with confidence. "Riley, He redeemed it all. He gave you Josh even when you didn't need or know you wanted him. Then you had Greyson and look at the gift he is!"

She shared how she sees Christ in me through it all. My heart is for Jesus, never stopping. While that is true, out of sheer desperation, I do not understand how she can see that and think anything good. Apparently, she had already shared my story in order to minister to a friend in need. I'm so glad she did but when she told me what she said I started laughing hysterically! It was completely unimaginable for someone Godly to think of my story when trying to share something helpful.

It went something like this:

"I have a friend who got pregnant before she was married. It was two people who loved Jesus but they made a mistake. They never let it change their relationship with the Lord. They did the right thing and got married. They live a surrendered life and serve the Lord together."

Put it that way and it sounds so simple! I wish it were that easy! The truth is, my mistakes created shame and hiding and almost paralyzed me for a decade.

Also important to note that the baby was not the mistake she was referring to. "Babies happen," as I was bluntly told by my silk-flower florist for the wedding. Babies are absolutely love and grace bundled in joy.

Stefini's use of my life to bring love to someone else was in stark contrast to my own heart and the story in my mind and it all made me dizzy. I left that conversation so confused. When other people's words actually bring death or life and have for so long dictated my life, her words of deep deep value to me, because of her love and Godly perspective, birthed new life in me that day. I had never before been able to see my story as useful or encouraging. In my mind, I had tainted the whole Christian culture and brought shame on us all!

It took so much time to heal. Yes, I pursued Jesus and worshiped through it all but it was not without pain and stretching and healing. I'm not especially proud of it, though I do not know where I could have quickened the process. I wish I could change it. We do see people and think they should heal faster, trust more, believe the promises. Progress seems so slow! We see some walking in freedom and in healing and think it was quick and easy for them. But when you know someone, you understand the work it takes to forgive and renew the mind. That is why I laughed—I definitely didn't see myself as one who walks in their healing, making it look easy. Instead of just deciding to embrace the grace, I had to let Jesus touch that hurt and heal it at the deepest level.

> I had to let Jesus touch that hurt and heal it at the deepest level.

One time I was talking to someone else about our "big sins" and the comment to me was, "At least yours produced a miracle," speaking of my son. I am so proud of him. Hmmm, I really didn't know what to say to that then. Nothing could be truer. It begs the question: do all mistakes produce miracles? They have to.

More freedom given from this conversation full of being honest, facing hard things. God is rewriting the narrative of my heart to see that my life is not over. It is not too late. I didn't ruin everything. God doesn't see the condition of my life. He is attached to the beauty within that is a reflection of His love and divine purpose. Again, it is incredibly awkward talking about myself but so powerful knowing what someone else sees in me.

Look at this stuff, isn't it neat?
Wouldn't you think my collection's complete?
Wouldn't you think I'm the girl,
The girl who has everything?

The Little Mermaid

17

Tacos & Pregnant

"Why did you make tacos?" was Joshua's question immediately after I told him we were pregnant with our first baby. He was filled with compassion for me and wondered why I had suffered in silence until after I filled his belly. Didn't he know that's the only reasonable option when you're about to have a hard talk? Fill 'em up! That's what I do. I avoid hard things and first put on a show. Carefully sandwich in any negative layers, completely surrounded by creative ways to ease the situation, making it as gentle as possible.

We were sitting cross legged together on his bed. "I have to tell you something." He looked at me expectantly, already fearing what he knew was a possibility. I hope I didn't make him wait too long. "I'm pregnant." In that moment, we immediately broke as we faced the reality of a fallacy impossible to hide. Not exactly the way we would have chosen to spend a moment that should have been filled with joy.

Are expectations ever really met? Our best laid plans in piles. Isn't it years later you wonder what all the fuss was about? About anything really. I could have my eyes on a new pair of boots, it is all I can think about. I get the boots. A year, maybe two, passes and I don't care about the boots at all. Old news. Things feel so monumental in moments. When will I meet someone? When will I get this job? Does God want me to do this or that? Choices, waiting, longing, craving, hoping. So much time passes as we wish for the next thing. Then some things seem to break time, causing all else to fade with its powerful wave of 'this is happening' whether you want it to or not. They change the course of who you thought you were or who you will ever be, at least it seems so in the moment.

Humanity invades unbeckoned. Bellies swollen with new life don't hide. They force grace into your very being, bringing in love that is incomprehensible. Love undeserved. A love you didn't go looking for but one that fills every piece of you, changing your life dramatically, starting with belly kicks. I remember when Joshua and I were chilling in the living room and for the first time we could see our baby's foot move the skin across my belly. The love for that baby and the love that baby poured into us is indescribable. It broke a false sense of perfection in our lives and we realized that no matter how many times we think we understand how something is going—we have an illusion of control—we fall flat again and are carried by our Savior again, because His second chances never run out. Parenting never stops bringing us to that place.

My mom made up for the need for a joyful celebration; however, my parents' wait for the news was substantially lengthier. I couldn't make the words form in my mouth. We sat on the edge of their couch, not brown anymore. They finally retired from the military and upgraded their furniture as they settled into their permanent home, back in the city where they grew up. They waited patiently. I do not even know how Joshua, essentially a stranger to them, was brave enough or strong enough to sit beside me while offering me security, even then, as I cowered in fear. As soon as my mom heard the news that I was pregnant, she squealed with this unexpected exclamation, "We're having a baby!" I still can't think of a better response, because every baby deserves it. Relief swept the room. My dad also met us with gracious abundance, with the most humble, "I've messed up 857 times today, you've done this one thing."

What I would give for Joshua to have the fairy tale wedding he longed for, surrounded by his very best friends—and he has a lot because once you're Joshua Powell's friend, you always are. What I would give to present myself to him pure and full of life, without the weight of failed dreams. Turns out he really isn't to blame for my failed dreams, no matter how many times I try to blame him. If there was anything I could do differently, that's it. I would give him a dream life, though eighteen years in, I'm pretty sure he and I could agree over shared sushi that we are indeed living our dream life. Of course, not a detail is one we could have planned in advance. Life is so far beyond weddings and plans and expectations. There's a song about life being interesting when you have a story to tell at parties because you've lived a little. I like that thought. It's oddly comforting.

When we decided to marry quickly so we could welcome our baby boy into our home together, I actually already had the dress I needed for the dinner cruise reception. I had gotten it as I traveled through Georgia and stopped to reintroduce my full-grown self to Mrs. Janice, the Sunday school teacher who first introduced me to Jesus. Well she couldn't have known it, but she showed me Jesus all over again and for no reason at all gave me a fancy dress that fit just right that would be perfect for me when I needed it.

My husband and I have been gutted through and through like these old houses we share a love for. There is promise in holding space for what was and celebrating bringing in the new. And new we very much needed. But we've learned to appreciate our path. I think we really learned how to create life together with every wall demolition and every new light and board and trim. Build build build—we never stop building our life together. Perfection is a mirage. Who attains it? Why do we go after it so hard? Why do we hold others to it? I wish I could tell this story without eliciting judgment, but I can't and I'm okay with that. Jesus is my goal. Not perfection. Or impressing.

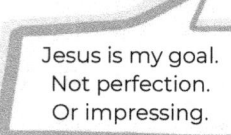

Jesus is my goal. Not perfection. Or impressing.

Although I still might wear a mini skirt on a date to get my man's attention! Though I'm confident he's more impressed with my ideas. He needs a chance to comment here, don't you think?

Through marriage, God is able to rewrite my narrative by teaching me I can be honest and still loved. It isn't silent and pretty that my husband longs for. He values my whole self and we've grown in our ability to say what is true. Intimacy only comes with trust and truth.

Unreserved, unrestrained
Your love is wild
Your love is wild for me
It isn't shy, it's unashamed
Your love is proud
To be seen with me
Cause You don't give Your heart in pieces
You don't hide Yourself to tease us
Uncontrolled, uncontained

Amanda Cook, Bethel Music, Pieces

18
Memories

In sixth grade, I was riding the school bus home one day from Hahira Middle School. That bus driver must have been a race car driver in his former years. He took those country roads at such a high speed our hair would be whipped around our faces. Every day we'd go on this long dirt road and there was a certain spot, where every day, we would catch air. The wheels of that bus had to fly over that dusty bump, because I know every single day my bottom came off the seat!

For whatever reason, on one particular day, I was made by the bus driver to sit on a seat of three people, so I was positioned ever so snugly between two girls who were not my friends. My memory of the level of my irritation with this situation has not faded with time. I was embarrassed to be in this seat and I did *not* like those people. I wanted to sit with my friends. During the bus ride, the girls on either side of me were acting completely obnoxious by continuously flicking the head of the boy on the bench in front of us. My annoyance grew by the second because he kept turning around asking who was flicking him until he finally lost all patience, turned around and slapped *me* across the face! ME! I wasn't even the one flicking him! I was the one who was thrust into a seat with dreadful people and forced to be a part of this dumb scenario.

Well, no one cared about that or the fact that no one had ever treated me that way before. I was taken to the principal's office and got in the biggest trouble of my whole eleven years. When I told my dad about that, he got really mad and marched up to the school to defend me. Of course, he was irate that his perfect little girl had been slapped. I was little. Even in sixth grade I was probably the size of a third grader. He was so mad at them until they told him that I had flicked that kid in the forehead... first. And then he was mad at me. The best part of the story is that for a lot of years we have told it and I have always adamantly denied lying about the facts that day. Forever I have told the story and when I tell the story, I say that I told my dad I flicked that kid on his forehead while saying in a mocking voice, "It was me! There! I'm the one who flicked you," but my *dad* in his fury missed that detail and let his emotions take over.

Until now. The proof is in the journal.

> Entry #32
> If I could go back in time I would tell the truth
> in sixth grade.
> I didn't tell my parents that I flicked him first.

The debate of my life has been set straight and somehow, in some fallible way, I was remembering it all wrong! In the same way, I had been wrongly remembering several hard years that I tried to erase from my life as having never happened. Bad memories are ingrained in our minds; like a zit, it's all you see.

Research shows we ruminate on negative experiences, giving them more attention, more language. Therefore they stick, even as we lose the good memories. This must be why God tells us to remember what He has done and to think on what is good, for the renewal of our minds.

Suddenly, I got to a place in my adult healed life where I didn't want to forget any years of my life anymore. It seemed there was more space for remembering. Surely, in all of that time, there were many beautiful things happening. I didn't want to forget that time with my brother and sister! I didn't want to forget all of the things I was good at or that I enjoyed. I wanted to be able to tell a story about my friends or something that happened in that season with a light heart and genuine happiness. I asked my parents to help me with this, so periodically I would just get a text from my dad with a picture and a memory and a note of what he thought about me. It was simple things that were so sacred, like how I made decorating the Christmas tree fun for him. I was a gracious gift receiver, loving to my siblings, because these were characteristics I had genuinely forgotten about myself. He has always told me who I am. It doesn't matter how old I get, I think I'll need him to keep reminding me. Remembering the right things must be one of the most important pieces to moving forward.

How amazing it is to be loved by my dad. Joshua and I had a couple over for dinner. The man spent a good amount of time with my dad. He told me that when they are at lunch they can be laughing and talking, but when my dad just says my name, he gets a lump in his throat and is swallowing the tears. They said I am absolutely his favorite person. They were laughing at me hysterically, as was Josh. I was so embarrassed! They said anyone can be on stage singing and my dad just stands there, but when I get up to sing he starts by putting his hands in his pockets and then he always ends up sitting and wiping away the tears from his face.

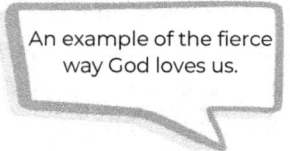

An example of the fierce way God loves us.

Goodness, to be loved like that. He loves all of my siblings that way and he loves my children with the same fierceness. His love certainly sets the example for the way God must look at us in amazement.

As I drove through the beach town I had tried so hard to forget, God sweetly showed me all the ways I had been brave and faithful to use my life for others. I had forgotten them all, like starting a business on my sixteenth birthday and hosting a successful launch party in a large corporate building. He reminded me that I had been employed and worked hard at a well-respected local business. I was president of the BCM Christian club at our college campus my freshman year, then I led worship in the band for hundreds of students. Those things can be shadowed by regret or they can be celebrated and enjoyed, because they were good fun things that I am so happy I got to do.

Something has changed within me
Something is not the same
I'm through with playing by the rules
Of someone else's game
Too late for second-guessing
Too late to go back to sleep
Its time to trust my instincts
Close my eyes and leap
Its time to try defying gravity

Wicked, Defying Gravity

19

Starting to See a Trend

At that point in my 'Rewrite Your Story' trips, I was definitely seeing a trend. "I'm onto you, God." Each person I shared my story with replaced a narrative in my mind, something I practiced thinking about myself and my past, with a new truth.

Everyone was carefully chosen by God to speak life, replacing old with new, flipping my belief system, and redefining my identity. I chose to believe those people who were carved into my life. These weren't strangers on the internet. These were real people who loved me and I trusted them completely. I chose to believe them and practiced believing the new truths. The kindness of God was written in so many details.

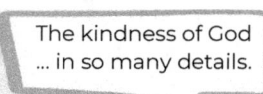
The kindness of God ... in so many details.

Unexpected... I say that as if all the previous conversations were expected. They totally were *not*. Nonetheless, unexpected truth-finding happened with a current friend, Summer. Her friendship is altogether unexpected. She is profound in every way. She has a way of seeing the best in every single child and adult, and the fact that I get to be her friend astounds me on a regular basis. The way she played a part in rewriting my story could be my favorite of all because it is so so so subtle. Every other person heard me and listened and responded with a powerful new truth to set my mind in peace. The only way I know to put this is Summer felt my heart in a connection beyond words. She became my friend later in life so all she knows is my account of the events. She wanted every single detail.

As I sat across from her in that Panera booth, she cried uncontrollably because her gift is an empathy that crosses normal lines. She felt my grief in her whole being. Honestly, at that point, I believe she felt it on my behalf, and she took it and held it as sacred. She saw beauty in something that felt dead to me. I was too numb to feel but her tears washed life into that story. I mean that with my whole heart. I've never experienced anything like that.

It's like my favorite movie, *Avatar*. Jake is asking what the connection with nature is like and Neytiri tells him it is a seeing that is a knowing. I'm not calling Summer divine because she would die of embarrassment, but all I'm saying is she has a gift that reflects the heart of the Father that I don't deserve. Time with her softened me, even if it did mean I looked at her awkwardly because she was crying tears I should have been crying and I didn't know what to say or do.

I had all but given up
Desperate for a sign from love
Something good, something kind
Bringing peace to every corner of my mind

Then I saw the garden
Hope had come to life
To sweep away the ashes
And wake me from my sleep

You will stop at nothing
To heal my broken soul

Kari Jobe, The Garden

20
God Doesn't Like Me

When we start to look for something, we see it.

A few years ago we started shopping for a new car to fit our growing family. Suddenly everywhere we looked we saw SUVs with a third row. How does the eye suddenly see something it hasn't seen before? It is known as frequency bias which just means that when you give something your attention, the frequency at which you notice it is heightened. I could apply this to any chapter of this book, but let's focus it here.

When we start to look for God, we start to find Him. Does that mean we can make up any thought, call it God, and start to see it? It kind of seems that way, but that isn't genuine; it lacks depth or integrity, and simply can't be sustained. It has no power.

So if that is what every Christian is doing, then we all have very strong minds and set our intentions each day on being who we want to be and manage to be successful... right? False. Obviously false. This isn't about pulling up our boots straps, or putting on our big girl panties, and choosing to be kind today. It isn't me before I walk into a crowded party hyping myself up to be friendly and funny and fun and everything I need to be. That falls flat. I've definitely done it many times but there is no energy.

So how does energy flow from God? How does creativity flow? Gifts? Life? We are talking about the fruit of the Spirit. And we are talking about a deeply rooted belief that comes with seeking and finding God, starting in your own story.

I didn't even realize my brother was on this infamous list and then he was, because he is a constant in my life. I need him always.

No matter what happened or where I was, where he was and what he thought about me, his presence in my life was integral. I carried significant grief and burden about various ways our relationship had gone and the ways I had impacted us.

In the military, my only constant was my family. I didn't grow attached to houses, schools, or friends. I was attached to my brother. I have memories with him in every house. In Tampa, it was being filthy in the sandpit in our backyard. In Illinois, it was filling our shirts with pebbles or jumping on the beds. In GA, it was roaming the neighborhood on our bikes and playing outside with friends for hours. In Sumter, SC, there were so many things, from Pizza Inn after youth group to playing Super Mario in our game room with its checkered flag wallpaper. My parents went all out. We shared friends and it was such a sweet season. In Florida, it was running out of gas on the way to school and cruising perfectly into a gas station as if we had planned it that way. It was filling the screened-in porch with the moving paper used to wrap our belongings and crashing into it like it was a pile of leaves. It was feeding our new baby sister candy for the first time. There was a season of going in our own directions, but we always came back and then we had kids the same age and it's the greatest dream come true I never knew I had.

So anyway, I went to Tyler's house and sat on the back porch with him and his wife, Allie, to catch them up on all the details. He had been so young and preoccupied with his own high school and college experience at the time that he really wasn't aware of much of what was going on. I'm honestly not sure he cared to hear the details, so it was a bit awkward but I shared anyway. He has always had to put up with all my shenanigans.

Ultimately, I walked away with a tall order questioning my belief that God loves me. I mean, I know the old song:

Jesus loves me, this I know,
For the Bible tells me so...

But I was questioning. Did He really love me? Did He even like me?

What does God say about *you?*

"If you are shamed by your story then you don't believe what God says about you." That was really, really shocking to hear, since I thought I loved God most. It was a definite first and not rosy like my friends' encouragements. It became the oldest following the younger in wisdom and with great adoration.

It was an area I needed to explore. What did I believe about how God saw me and how I saw myself? It was a moment of applying all that I had gathered and putting it to the test. The question became, "Can I love my story?"

The Lord bless you and keep you
Make His face shine upon you
And be gracious to you
The Lord turn His face toward you and give you peace
May His favor be upon you and a thousand generations
And your family and your children
And their children and their children

Chris Brown, Cody Carnes, and Steven Furtick,
The Blessing

21
I Am Human

Why do we choose what we know is hurting us?

Does it have to do with belief?

Does it have to do with not listening? Not taking time to listen?

Is it because we believe this is the best there is?

Or that we are somehow responsible for making life good enough? Responsible for better?

Unbelief, a limiting mindset, and false beliefs rob you from your potential and life in a different way from how doubt does. These were my ceiling. Unbelief was the trap making me feel small.

I did a study once, by Beth Moore of course, called *When Godly People Do Ungodly Things.* It resonated at my core because I carried so much guilt for constantly messing up when I knew better.

When I started this whole journey, I went to lunch with my dad and I was telling him about my goals and my new willingness to follow God wherever He would lead, but that I was facing a big struggle, a block. I was sitting across the booth from him eating our favorite: calamari. I could see out the windows but it seemed like all he had to look at was me, so he was expectantly listening. I felt really antsy and like I wanted some kind of breakthrough, but it was all energy with no direction. I couldn't really put words to what I thought then, but as I floundered through, finally the truth of it sort of emerged. I can remember saying something about how lots of people do dumb things, make mistakes, go through hell. Honestly, people experience much worse things that are impossible to live with. Every person I follow who tells their horror story from stage, or writes a book, and speaks of God's redeeming love is telling something tragic that happened *to them* in their childhood or their past. Someone else was horrible to them, through no fault of their own.

For some of us, it feels like everything that is wrong in life is our own fault. I'm one of those. I am completely to blame. I was a Christian. I knew a better way. I chose wrong. That may not tell the full story. I am not completely to blame for any of the "trauma" in my life. I do understand that and accept it and have processed it. Nonetheless, everything that happened was after I was already a Christian and it was all the result of my choices. I was fully loved by my parents and had all the tools to be successful. There is this expectation spoken and unspoken that Christians act like they claim: "walk the talk". Somehow we get in the church and forget that we are amongst humans.

My sister and I went backpacking. It was my first experience carrying 30 lbs through the wilderness with no plan of where to sleep and eating food out of dried packs; actually, it was one of my first experiences with camping in general. I love to hike and I had grown to really absorb a lot of energy from this environment amongst trees and views. The simplicity. The lack of expectations.

Now I told Bree I would only go if the weather were perfect, but as the time drew closer my weather app was not telling me what I needed to hear. Temperatures in the thirties and rain were predicted. Bree was steadfast—"We're going."—but also dependent on my agreement. My head went round and round. '*Do I go and be tough and committed to this adventure? Obviously I can do hard things. I need to be tough.*'

Then, '*I am thirty-five years old! There is zero reason I have to go on this trip. If the weather is bad then I should cancel and wait for a better time. It is just plain stupid to go out into the wilderness during a blizzard and risk freezing to death. Who would choose that? No one is making me. I just have to MAKE A CHOICE!*'

So the night before we left, we had to choose how much clothing to take. With the unpredictable weather, we would need clothes to get wet, plus dry clothes, extra shoes, rain gear, and stuff for cold weather. Layers, layers, layers, which means more weight to carry for every single one of the twenty-three miles.

The next morning, we were driving across the state headed toward Forney Ridge Trail in North Carolina and I was reading up on how to react in the unwelcome sighting of a bear and differentiating between different bears. If you see brown do this; if you see black...

So we got a later start and were at the trailhead late in the afternoon; driving up the mountain on a steep and narrow two-lane highway. I could not see the mountain wall directly to my right because of the thick fog blanketing the mountain. It was terrifying and thrilling. I'm sure I talked entirely too much as my nerves battled to take over. We parked at the top of the mountain at a trailhead that began in a public parking lot, but the view was completely obscured by fog. Everywhere you looked for 360 degrees was only dense moisture, and it was freezing. Thank you, February. But here we go. Balls to the wall. Reckless. Brave. One of us felt reckless and the other brave and I was committed to her twenty-two-year-old self so let's go. '*If she wants to go then I'm in*.' And off we went to stepping... for three days.

We were probably two miles into the creaky forest where the fog had found even the deepest crevices—I mean it: you couldn't see much of anything—when Bree stopped solid in front of me. I bumped into her coming to an abrupt halt. I could hear her whispering lowly and it took me a good second to know what she was saying. And then it was apparently clear. "Bear, bear, bear, bear," and she was backing up into me. There to the right of the trail, not too close, but very much close enough, stood a black bear. And it was looking at us. Do we go forward? Do we stay still? Do we run back? I mean, truth be told we didn't want to backtrack! The twenty plus miles still ahead would be hard enough without doing any backtracking. We wanted to move forward. I remembered my research. If you see a black bear, tell it you are human. So I yelled the only thing that came to mind, "I am human!" The obvious.

I am human. I am human. Huuuuuuu-maaaaaan! Fully human. I am not super. I am not the elect. I am not divergent or Ariel or any other fictional character where an author gets to decide a happy ending. I am fallible and I made a choice and it ended in some pain. The question I can't seem to outrun is: "Does my humanity thwart God's plan? Did I miss it? Is my best plan ruined?" I lived as if this were true and in full despair for more than a decade.

My level of pain and humiliation paralleled my level of pride. The worship of self.

I thought I could do whatever I wanted and it not hit me like a truck. I thought I could choose the wild and fun life all while maintaining a posture of humility and grace, representing the one who is love. I thought I could have the best intention but not sacrifice any of my desires. I thought I could have it all.

The weight of sin is death and there are moments it seems I feel the full weight of it.

But also I am merely human and so I am going to make choices and instead of completely drowning in the guilt of it all, I can allow them to shape me and guide me, trusting they are wrapped in grace.

I can make a choice, wrong or right, and then keep going with whatever consequence that comes. It doesn't end the world. Mine or anyone else's.

Speaking those words unlocked a truth in me. The words rang with power to warn the bear, though honestly he seemed unimpressed by our caution. The bear basically looked like he already knew the stated obvious. He set the tone, unbothered, so we proceeded. We didn't see any more bears on that trip, but kept our eyes peeled in the craggy forest. Honestly, the whole trip felt like a real-life game of Candy Land. By the way, Bree was an incredible trail guide, food provider, fire and tent maker. She kept me alive and I kept her entertained, possibly annoyed, as I narrated the Candy Land game all along the way. That night was a full moon, and we were on high alert for all the fellow humans entering the woods for rituals and such. The bear became the least of our concerns! When I think of Bree and our time together my heart absolutely bursts. I do not have words that can hold my immense love for her.

The words, I am human, bore witness to something much deeper and cracked something solid inside me wide open. I think it had something to do with space. My whole journey has been about space. Space for a new perspective, an added option in the multiple choices.

Being human was never an option for me. That wasn't on the list. Failing wasn't on the list. It wasn't a possibility. That sounds silly, ridiculous, but it's very very honest.

So what do I do with this realization that I am human?

Acknowledging humanity, imperfections, allowed me to accept them as expected, useful even. When I work out, I want to push through a challenge so I can feel proud and strong. It has become some of that for me in healing. I crave a breakthrough. I want to be in the moment fully so that I can experience the light, the presence of God, and the gift that comes on the other side of facing something with honesty.

Our goal isn't perfection. Rather, it is a surrendered heart for the purpose of connection. It is freedom found in God's goodness. So when I started to see my mistakes as just a part of living, I found their value and allowed grace to attach there. Grace settled in over the details and allowed them to grow beauty where before there was only dense fog hiding the life. There were only threats lurking in the shadows threatening to pull me down. When I faced my weaknesses and gave them space, I removed the threats. I exposed the dark things to light and their power faded. There became an understanding that the pieces of myself that feel less than bundled with grace and love are undeniably dynamic moves of God that shatter anything threatening to interfere.

We present ourselves clothed how we want to be perceived. Covered in deep layers making ourselves invisible. Scantily begging to be seen; richly needing to be important. We dress ourselves up to portray whatever image we think serves us best.

What we don't usually choose is to be naked. I hate being naked. Neck-ed, Nay-ked. How do you say it? Tutsie or tootsie? Pecan or pecahn? Up to you! But being neck-ed—because that's how I say it and I'll defend it forever!—most don't choose that and the Sloan family least of all. We prefer that tough exterior of hard-earned perfection. So when God called me to share my story, I assumed it would be of my shining magnificence. Of how much I loved him and pleased him! I had no idea it would be absolutely gut wrenching and that I would in fact loathe the story and spend ten-plus years trying to hide it. Make it shrink. Go away. Anything but broadcast it on all platforms.

When Life and Beliefs Collide gets quickly to the heart when it describes the woman's encounter with Jesus. We all call her the woman at the well, as if that is her whole name. I wish I could just share the whole chapter in this book!

"His omniscience assured Him that no new revelations about her private life would ever change His mind about her. He already knew all. By the time the conversation was over, she was a different woman—not covered with shame but dressed with theology. Theology is for women. It is practical. It nurtures, transforms, and shapes a woman's life and her ministry to others."

We must wear our beliefs boldly, clothed in grace and strength. This brings God into the visible moments of our days. This is what takes us from looking over our to-do list and wondering where God fits to a settled heart breathing Him in and out, settled in a peace that literally carries us from glory to glory, all the while the baby is demanding, the kids are complaining, and the teenager is choosing his own way. The husband has no time to put toward creative effort in marriage, because of the three things already listed, amongst many others. Let's be honest, neither do I!

Rather than be shaken by all of these moving parts, or maybe dull parts, we sink into a presence that stills the heart; the awareness of presence stills the heart. Presence of God breathes life and clarity into every situation. Be clothed in goodness. I traded my shame face for identity. Instead of clothing myself, I allow the Father to cover and provide. My theology shifted drastically in this year of adventure to realize that "too good to be true" was a lie. He pulled me boldly into the Kingdom where I belong and where I am favored, fully known and welcomed with joy! A different woman. A settled woman.

Here is the punch line in this comedy: Shame was masked in a million ways all over my story, but God slowly and lovingly unveiled truth, with gentle kindness, reminding me of who I really am. This journey wasn't entirely about finding me or me telling my story. I realized it was about God telling His. The story is about seeing God there, where He has always been in every detail, pursuing. It is so different from me loving Him with such exuberant ambition. Rather, it is me surrendering to His love and giving permission for Him to help me and be a part of my days.

As I learn to hold my humanity and live in the spiritual realm, I face a constant and tense duality. We need God and want Him, as we experience the wholeness He offers, but often choose independence from Him. Choosing to follow Jesus is a giving of my life, my image, my pride. Yet, in His kindness, His invitation to bring our weakness is so that He can carry it, so that He can give me strength. So that He can use every broken thing as if it were beautiful. In desperation, I rip off the cloth that binds me in hiding, and I choose to be known. To get real in humility, in surrender. This exposing of our very own humanity is laying down our lives, joining in suffering, trusting in the resurrection.

> He invites you to lay it all down... and He makes you new.

Romans 13:11 (TPT)
Time to wake up! Remove what is done in darkness like filthy clothes, clothe ourselves with the radiance of light as our weapon.

In order to be strong, I owned my weakness. To be free, I exposed my chains. To reach perfection, I loosened my grip on striving and impossible expectations. I realized that God had not set these expectations for me. When I look to Him, I am completely where I'm meant to be and everything is working for me. He is for me, pleased, and guiding, confident in the end result. He is not rushed or worried. He doesn't feel behind and He certainly is not worried about what has been wasted because His whole breath is one of restoration. He does not allow life to be stolen or moments to be wasted. He clothes. He covers and provides. He leads the way to a resurrected life.

You are my treasure, my reward
My heart delights in who You are
Consider me Your offering
Cause I was made to bless You, Lord
You are my one thing
Jesus, You're my one thing
You are my own thing
Jesus, You're my one thing
You're so much better than the rest

Kalley Heiligenthal, Better Than the Rest

22
Resurrection Day

I can hear it and feel it on the pages. From the start, I was wrestling, wrestling, fighting for breath, digging through weeds, unsure of where I was going. Like swimming in the pond with no direction, no way out. It didn't matter that people were yelling at me to swim. I swam and swam and swam myself into exhaustion, but I was drowning in shame.

It feels like I chased down tragedy, ignoring red flags. How can there be comedy in that? I'm completely relieved to see clearly Jesus chased me down faster. He was there in every step. As I sought truth and went back for a fact check, what I found was so much laughter, so much grace, so many treasures and surprises. The comedy is I don't even recognize that girl. She didn't believe she was worth pursuing. She thought she was too far gone. Floating in the world without a tether, having to hold on tight to every string she could find that would keep her in the crowd. Keep her in the church she loves. Everything changed when she landed and there was ground: ground that gives with a bounce, ground that settles and propels.

As we walk through our lives we can face tension while keeping our heart open. We can stand firmly planted in an unchanging promise that God is for us even as we grapple with things that are out of our control. How can we do both? It's life-changing wisdom to grasp the slightest depth of how to hold the tension of humanity with the longing of heaven and even the holding of heaven, as we are promised we do even in the absence of seeing or feeling it very often. We can present ourselves surrendered to God, making space to let His love wash over us, transforming us. It is the essence of who we are, holding space for heaven on earth. How can I be so broken and have purpose? How can I have ruined every goal I had for myself and yet be successful because of who I am? Who God says I am?

Golly! Holy smokes. Look at what my life was!

Just because one is capable does *not* mean they are responsible. I lived for years saying, "I'm handling all of this well, and I don't see anyone else signing up, so I am just going to keep on." I worked three jobs most of our marriage, went to grad school with a baby, remodeled three houses, built a new house, and supported my husband through grad school and two back surgeries. The list is endless and was I happy? Well, I wanted to be. Those were happy things. My mom asked me that powerful question once, "Riley, are you happy?" In that moment my heart cracked open with a glimpse of truth sneaking out unbidden.

Maybe you need permission to seek. Can I ask you: are you happy? Are you?

Of course you are. You are doing so many things that make you feel alive, or at least have an illusion of looking alive. So many happy things, you have no reason or excuse to complain. That wouldn't be very Godly.

Wait a second. Are you happy? I'm really asking.

There was a week in our lives a few years ago that stands out to me more than any other week. It wasn't even about my life, but it changed it in a huge way. It was a story on Instagram. Here are how the posts went:

We're asking for prayer. Day 1.
    I had to go back to read this post later to understand the urgency.

I keep seeing this same image of a toddler shared in everyone's stories. Day 2.
    What is going on?

It's a good day for a resurrection. Day 3.

I got really curious. Why does she keep talking about this? Can you even ask for one?

It's a good day for a resurrection. Day 4.

Oh, it is for her daughter. I've never ever seen one person so boldly ask and definitely never seen someone make themselves so vulnerable for the entire world to see.

It's a good day for a resurrection. Day 5.

By now the whole world is watching. Waiting. Bated breath. Starting to believe. A hope is birthing as we lean into a belief we didn't let ourselves consider before. Something of the spirit, a world we rarely catch a glimpse of. The beyond. Looking for life. Looking for a real response from a real God in Heaven.

This mama laid it all out for her baby. Hoped fully. Believing. Broken. Desperate. She bravely let us watch.

Watching her grieve and heal into someone new in tiny Instagram squares for three years has shown me a new way to live. A new way to cling to the one who is better. Her Olive is dancing with Jesus and she openly longs for the day they are together. She shares her longings for Heaven, but she also sees the world differently. She lives differently and it's impossible to describe, but honestly it feels like Eden must feel. Her connection is sweet, tainted with grief. It resembles more yearning for the eternal than it does someone distraught. She steps one foot in Heaven, while gravity pulls her to Earth. Duality. She makes this connection, this dance with Jesus, look possible. Tangible. She has a supernatural way of putting words to the things of the spirit, which allows me to feel it, long it for it, too.

Just as she invited us all to resurrection, sweet friend, today is a great day for a resurrection. So many of us are walking around as if we are dead. We have the opportunity to live. We still have time. It's not too late, We aren't too far gone. We didn't ruin it. Say yes, at any point, inviting heaven to earth in your life. Inviting connection with God into your today is possible.

God has made space for this story to be shared. This is never how I thought I would be known. Unlike the way I would dream my life to go, life is a battlefield. Nothing is easier or cleaner because I'm "on mission." Quite contrary, all hell breaks loose when you zone in with purpose to connect and be real.

I feel tender talking about my baby girl as I share how another mama had to let hers go for a while. Life is so incredibly hard at times and certainly some things are way harder than others. Some people face things that are unimaginable and I in no way feel worthy of sharing their story. Yet I can think of no more sacred way to offer life than to demonstrate the faith of a mother who fought to bring life into the world only to fight to keep her.

I had to let the idea of having a baby girl of my own go. I had to in order to survive. Before releasing it, I had clung to the idea of her every day, never fully present where I was. I had secretly wanted her for so long. I begged God to give her to me but deeply believed He couldn't trust me with a girl. I had not been worthy enough to raise a daughter. I had messed up the chance for that. Something must be wrong with me if He knows I can't handle a girl. I wouldn't be a good girl mom. Ultimately she was given out of a belief I didn't deserve her, so absolutely she is the assurance of a God who makes this connected dance in Eden possible.

Don't get me wrong, I looooooove being a boy mom. My boys are my heart throb. They melt me. Both of them in completely different ways. I'm not trying to be dramatic or suck up because I'm talking about the girl. They absolutely cause me to swoon.

It's not so much something that my boys don't give me as it is a belief that God was withholding something special from me. It felt like the ultimate punishment for all that I had done wrong. It's kind of that idea that I don't have a beautiful wedding dress for a girl anyway. In my head I accepted it as a natural consequence. These kinds of thinkings in our heads don't have to make sense because they never will. Our heads just think things they shouldn't.

And then she was given. We sat together on the couch to open the letter I had picked up from the hospital that concealed her gender. We had done the early blood work, because good grief, I was considered geriatric in this unexpected pregnancy. The perk of this was knowing whether our miracle baby was a boy or a girl. The baby is healthy, page one. Page two, scan scan scan, so many words, there it is. Female. I hit him, because that is what I do if I am mad, happy, or sad. We sat in silence, smiles on our faces, weird smiles, crooked with disbelief, unsure what to think. Tears streaming down my face. The Lord sees me. He doesn't hate me after all. Even if He hadn't given this baby, He is still the One I cling to and have come to believe the absolute best about. Even if He never gives me another good gift, I know He is the one who saves. The one who comforts and gives life. She is Ivy, persevering into unexpected places. Growing from a place of contentment and trust.

It is the absolute earth-shaking, mind-blowing truth that the God who is above all and in all created life to be lived as humans so that in our humanity, He could make all things new. He took what I considered ruined and turned it into a fairy tale. My life is new. My mind is new. I have something to give, but I'm not attached to that anymore. I crave time on the floor in the presence of God. I may not be dancing like that mom at the 'spend the night' party so long ago, but my kids see me in the presence of God on a regular basis. They know that He is my source of peace and the fuel for my life. Sometimes I wear a robe, like my parents. It's literally so gross, but I hope my kids will remember it and know that I followed after the Lord, who settles our lives. He is the one who gives them belonging.

All moms fight to bring their babies into the world; moms adopting fight most of all. We spend all the years raising them, laboring. The laboring of a mother is never over. Once we are independent from our parents, we take up our own fight. We learn to seek and find in new ways, unique ways, respond to whatever event or call is in our lives. We fall into traps and routines. We let weeds crowd. Ultimately, we all end up needing a resurrection.

Maybe we don't get to choose how the resurrection will appear. Though my healing is complete in Jesus, the resurrection of my story is still happening. In layers. I love to think of Jesus coming back to life in that tomb. Breath filling his lungs first, each flattened air sac popping open filled with life, the heart starting to beat, pulsing blood to his fingers and they start to wiggle, legs slowly stretch out, toes wiggling, like we do when we wake each morning. His eyes must have opened, as human eyes do, and maybe he soaked in that moment, reconnected to life, looking at his hands and feet. Every word spoken now fulfilled. Resurrection must feel like a dream coming true, almost like I've been here before in my imagination. I can't imagine He sprung from the rock as if he were late and in a hurry. It must have been slow, full of peace, right and good, as He awakened to the sensations.

Waking my kids is hard but I surely know how they feel. My husband wakes me and I without fail say, "I'm awake." He doesn't believe me, but I mean it. I'm awake, but I'm thinking first. I'm noticing. I'm pointing my toes and stretching my hips. He rubs my back one more time, just to make sure. "Good morning, Beautiful."

Resurrecting sometimes starts like that: on the inside where no one can tell anything is moving yet. The outside is covered in grief and going through motions. The outside is still walled up, guarded by rock.

Then the rock rolls away and Jesus says, "Let's go together. Let's come out of hiding and do something new. Let's create and heal and dance. Let's show the truth. Let someone see your scars, sweet girl. I want them to know all that is available to them."

Kalley Heiligenthal, mommy to sweet little Olive, echoes it best:

"It's time for her to come alive."

References

Chapter 1: Wake Up!
1. Evanescence. (2003). Bring Me to Life. Recorded by Evanescence. On *Fallen*. Wind-up.

Chapter 2: Belonging
1. Hillsong Worship. (2018). Touch of Heaven. Hillsong Worship. On *There is More: Instrumental*. Hillsong Capitol CMG.

Chapter 3: Good Girl vs. Bad Girl
1. Lewis, C. (1998). Not the Same. Live @ the Woodlands.

Chapter 4: Grand Plans
1. Needham, J. (2012). Clear the Stage. Originally Recorded by King, R. (2002). On *And All the Decorations Too*. Released by Needham, J. On *Clear the Stage*. Inpop Records.
2. Niequist, S. (2017). *Present Over Perfect: Leaving behind frantic for a simpler, more soulful way of living*. Center Point Large Print.

Chapter 5: Delight Delivery Girl
1. Elevation Rhythm. (2020). Quiet. Recorded by Elevation Rhythm. On *Quiet*. Elevation Worship Records.
2. Rohr, R., Chase, J., & Traeger, J. (2018). *Richard Rohr: Essential teachings on love*. Orbis Books.

Chapter 6: Meeting Joshua
1. Larson, J. (2005). Seasons of Love. From *Rent: Original Motion Picture Soundtrack*. El Dorado Studios. Skywalker Sound. Warner Bros.

Chapter 7: No Fear

1. Smith, T., Crocker, M., Houston, J. (et. al.) (2013). Oceans (Where Feet May Fail). Hillsong United. On *Zion*. Hillsong. Capitol CMG.
2. Moore, B. (2024). *Chasing Vines: Finding your way to an immensely fruitful life*. Tyndale Momentum.

Chapter 8: My Best Yes

1. Anderson-Lopez, K., & Lopez, R. (2019). Into the Unknown. Recorded by Idina, M., & Aurora. On *Frozen II (Original Motion Picture Soundtrack)*. Walt Disney.
2. Niequist, S. (2017). *Present over perfect: Leaving behind frantic for a simpler, more soulful way of living*. Center Point Large Print.
3. Maguire, G. (2006). *Wicked*. Headline Review.

Chapter 9: Walk in the Dark

1. Anderson-Lopez, K., & Lopez, R. (2019). Let It Go. Recorded by Idina, M., & Aurora. On *Frozen (Original Motion Picture Soundtrack)*. Walt Disney.

Chapter 10: Time to Rebuild

1. Battistelli, F. (2018). Defender. Recorded by Gretzinger, S. On *Own It*. Bethel Music.

Chapter 11: Design Your Life

1. McFerrin, B. (1988). Don't Worry Be Happy. Recorded by McFerrin, B. On *Simple Pleasures*. EMI-Manhattan.

Chapter 12: About Doubt

1. Needham, J.. (2012). Clear the Stage. Originally Recorded by King, R. (2002). On *And All the Decorations Too*. Released by Needham, J. On *Clear the Stage*. Inpop Records.
2. James, C. C. (2001). *When life and beliefs collide: How knowing god makes a difference*. Zondervan.

Chapter 13: Church Hurt

1. Jobe, K. (2017). Speak to Me. Recorded by Jobe, K. On *The Garden*. Bethel Music.
2. Buechner, F. (1977). *Telling the truth: The gospel as tragedy, Comedy, and Fairy tale*. Harper & Row.

Chapter 14: Another Drive

1.   Maverick City Music. (2019). Communion. Recorded by Gretzinger, S. & Lake, B. On *Maverick City Vol. 2*. Maverick City Music.

Chapter 15: More to the Story

1.   Smith, T., Crocker, M., Houston, J. (et. al.) (2013). Oceans (Where Feet May Fail). Hillsong United. On *Zion*. Hillsong. Capitol CMG.

Chapter 16: Babies Happen

1.   Riddle, J. L. (2009). Revelation Song. Recorded by Jobe, K. On *Kari Jobe*. Integrity Media. Gateway Create Publishing.

Chapter 17: Tacos & Pregnant

1.   Ashman, H., & Menken, A. (1989). Part of Your World. Recorded by Benson, J. On *The Little Mermaid: Original Motion Picture Soundtrack*. Walt Disney.

Chapter 18: Memories

1.   Gretzinger, S. (2016). Pieces. Recorded by Cook, A. On *Have It All*. Bethel Music.

Chapter 19: Starting to See a Trend

1.   Menzel, H. & Chenoweth, K. (2003). Defying Gravity. Recorded by Michele, L. On *Wicked: Original Cast Recording*. Universal Pictures.

2.   James Cameron, James Horner, James Horner & James Horner, N. D. (2009). Avatar. USA/UK.

Chapter 20: God Doesn't Like Me

1.   Jobe, K. (2017). The Garden. Recorded by Jobe, K. On *Kari Jobe Studio Album*. Sparrow Records, KAJE.

2.   Emerson, L. O. (1873) Jesus Loves Me. Boston: Ditson & Co., Oliver. [Notated Music] Retrieved from the Library of Congress, https://www.loc.gov/item/2023819173.

Chapter 21: I Am Human

1.   Carnes, C., & Jobe, K. (2020). The Blessing. Recorded by Carnes, C., & Jobe, K. On *Graves Into Gardens*. Elevation Worship Records.

2.   Moore, B. (2007). *When godly people do ungodly things: Arming yourself in the age of seduction*. Walker Large Print.

Chapter 22: Resurrection Day

1. Heiligenthal, K. (2023). Better Than the Rest. Recorded by Heiligenthal, K. & Funk, D. On *Better Than the Rest*. Bethel Music.

Additional Resources

If you want to go even deeper and take the journey with God to rewrite *your* story, I want to invite you to get the *Let's un-Do This: Rewrite Your Story Workbook.* This is my gift to you for reading my story and taking this journey with me.

Go to: *rileysloanpowell.com/gift.*

Scripture Index

About the Author

Riley is a speaker and bestselling author as well as a wife and mother to three amazing children. Through a pivotal journey back through her story, she changed the narrative of her life to become rooted in the truth that God loves her deeply. Now she uses all she has learned to lead others in finding their identity without performance, perfection, or exhaustion, and to learn how to hear God's voice in their own lives.

Learn more at: *rileysloanpowell.com*.

Thank You!

Thank you so much, dear friend, for taking the time to read my story. I pray it blessed you and encouraged you and inspired you in your own relationship with God. Would you take just a moment and leave your honest review on the book page? It would be of immense value to me and it helps more people to read the book!

Go to: *amazon.com/dp/B0CVNLGTST.*

www.ingramcontent.com/pod-product-compliance
Lightning Source LLC
Chambersburg PA
CBHW070658130626
46553CB00005B/1761